FROM OVERWHELMED

TO "I GOT THIS"

Guaranteed Success Route to Directing

Your Childcare Center

Carrie Casey &

Kate Woodward Young, M.Ed

From Overwhelmed to "I Got This"
Guaranteed Success Route to Directing Your Childcare Center

Copyright © 2021 by Carrie Casey
ISBN 978-1-954885-12-7 paperback
978-1-954885-11-0 ebook

Published by: CEY Press

Contents

Introduction

We are so glad to be here with you and share the steps to building your professional foundation for directing an early childhood or youth program.

After speaking with many of those whom we have worked with over the years - as coaching clients, friends and colleagues – we recognize the frustration that you feel when you're not ready for the world. We are so blessed to have figured out a way to help you.

You have this massive job. You are the cheerleader, CEO, nurse, counselor, CTO, marketing department, auditor, evaluator, substitute, oarsman, helmsman, clown, coach, HR manager, oracle, mentor & I don't know what all else for your program. It is a LOT! We have been in your shoes. They aren't comfortable.

Together with our help in this book and the accompanying workbook, you will go from overwhelmed to a certainty that you can do this!

This system has been a long time in the making. In many ways the information we are going to share with you has been handed down to us. It has come to us so clearly and effortlessly – which has been such a learning experience itself - because often we think to create something, it must be hard and/or a struggle.

It doesn't. You can learn from us as we learned from others. Let us be your coaches, your mentors.

Whether you are brand new in your position, you came to this program because your program has an issue that is overwhelming, or you've been procrastinating on something and are looking to move forward professionally, or you're very experienced and ready to get out on your own, this book is for you. We promise you will discover some strategies, tips, and new methodologies for thinking, along with tools to help move your future forward again and again.

If you are like Carrie and you hate writing in books, we have some help for you. We have made a companion workbook that has workbook pages, supplementary material, and plenty of room to write. Just go to TexasDirector.org/workbook.

That is one of the key things about this book. We are providing something that you will be able to use repeatedly when new things arise in your professional career. We will be sharing with you in detail different tools to use in your program. We promise if you show up and do the work you will build a solid foundation!

This book and its companion are meant to be tools. As tools, you pick them up over and over when needed. When everything is going well, it will go back to sitting on a shelf, collecting dust. But then one day you realize that the energy of your school has gone to pot, or that you are working 16 hours days, or that your enrollment is in the toilet. Get the book back out and use the tools. Get them dirty.

While you will be doing the work in this program independently, we do want to hear from you and learn about your progress and the intention that you have for yourself. If you need more support, we have coaching, training & mentoring programs available. No question is too small or anecdote too silly! Please send us email at any time to Carrie@TexasDirector.org or Kate@TexasDirector.org.

We wish you great success in your professional growth.

Carrie & Kate

SECTION I

CHAPTER 1

How Should Children Be Educated?

"The ideal condition would be, I admit, that men should be right by instinct, but since we are all likely to go astray, the reasonable thing is to learn from those who can teach."–Sophocles

There is no one answer to this question. There are hundreds if not thousands. Fortunately, we are not worried about all these different ways in which education has been envisioned. We are concerned with how you envision it now.

Many have likened education to shepherding sheep. The picture is usually of a rugged-looking guy or gal with a trusty border collie, trotting along some lush countryside while directing the sheep to wherever the shepherd wants them to go. So, if we use this analogy, you as the childcare director are the shepherd, the teacher is the border collie, and the sheep are the children. That must be the way it works, right? That has been the way it has always worked in the past, and people do love their comfort zones. "Just so **long as *the sheep get to where they need to go and are protected from dangers along the way***," they reason, "well then, that's just fine." And so, the tradition continues.

But then we watch a movie like *Babe,* which captures our attention as well as our hearts. All of a sudden, the paradigm shifts. A pig is standing in for the collie—Is that permissible? Is it okay? Is it possible and perhaps even profitable to guide the sheep in ways other than how folks have done it before?

On all counts, the answer is a resounding yes.

First, you need to take a few minutes and figure out what your idea of early childhood education really is. The good news is that it does not have to match up with any of the big-name educational philosophies like Montessori or Waldorf. So right now, get up and grab an empty journal, legal pad, or the accompanying workbook. Across the top of the first page, I want you to write in bold letters, "*Your Name* Educational Philosophy." Yep, I'm completely serious.

At this point some might be rolling their eyes, and I feel you. It drove me bananas every time an education professor asked me to do this. Didn't we basically think the same? After all, we were working in the same industry and learning at the same university.

But by the end of it, I discovered the weirdest thing: no two educational philosophies ever matched. Back in the olden days when I went to school, I didn't understand why this exercise was so important, and no one bothered to explain it to me. Time and experience brought these lessons home over and over again, and here they are in a nutshell:

> As a teacher, I needed to identify my own educational philosophy in order to *definitively know if I matched well with the school I worked for or wanted to work for.* As a leader, I needed to identify my own educational philosophy in order to *definitively explain my program's focus to new teachers and parents who looked to me for support and guidance.*

All of a sudden, the Susie Smith Educational Philosophy doesn't sound so outlandish, does it?

Before we start our lists, let's benefit from glancing inside some basic frameworks from the most influential designers in early childhood education.

Friedrich Fröbel (1782-1852)

Fröbel created the concept of kindergarten, recognizing that children have unique needs and abilities that differ from those of adults. He was fascinated by the concept of *development, not just learning:* how children must shift from one stage to another through the course of childhood. Since they must develop the attributes of the next stage of development over time, he concluded that the type of materials supplied in a child's environment both support and encourage these transitions. Spending much of his adult life working in academia, Fröbel educated families about the importance of play, games, and materials designed to help young children explore concepts. Specifically, he recommended that a child's free play should be spent singing, dancing, gardening, and engaging in self-directed play with learning materials. These materials he created are called Fröbel's gifts, which include the forerunners of modern wooden unit blocks.

Rudolf Steiner (1861-1925)

Steiner is credited with the Waldorf educational philosophy, which focuses on *head, heart, and hands*—thinking, feeling, and doing. Here a child's magical thinking and imagination are allowed to enliven these early childhood years, and the teacher is key in creating an interactive environment filled with new stories and artistic techniques.

The early childhood Waldorf program centers on experiential learning fostered through immersive, all-consuming activities such as dramatic play. Generally, the daily routine includes free play, art, circle time, practical life, and outside play in a homelike setting. The classroom itself is designed to be as aesthetically appealing as possible, focusing on natural materials and avoiding plastic or technology.

Dr. Maria Montessori (1870-1952)

Dr. Montessori launched the method that bears her name and is still practiced in over 20,000 schools around the world, including the one in your own neighborhood. A physician who ended up focusing on early childhood education, Montessori mirrored Fröbel as she observed the natural progression of children's development and understood that supplying the children with designed materials could aid in acquiring new skills and knowledge. To Montessori, *the environment is the primary teacher.*

She also highlighted the importance of self-directed play, asserting that "play is the work of the child." Her extensive materials build upon Fröbel's and are grouped into different categories: practical life, sensorial, science, mathematics, language, and culture.

Like Waldorf, the materials are generally wooden, ceramic, or glass. One of Montessori's concepts is the self-correcting activity: children learn that if they do not use the material as intended, then the activity cannot be completed. For instance, if a child wants to build a large tower with the pink cubes and puts a small one in before a larger one, the tower will naturally fall over. Lesson learned.

Loris Malaguzzi (1920-1994)

Malaguzzi is the last of our luminaries, hailing from the Italian city of Reggio Emilia. His philosophy emphasized *listening to the 100 languages of children.* Much like Waldorf, he thought children should have an immersive educational experience but grounded in the physical world rather than the imaginary. His philosophy is interchangeably referred to as Emergent Curriculum or simply Reggio. In a Reggio program, the teacher's role is to introduce new topics that they think might spark the children's interest and be ready with resources to feed that interest. If the children take a different direction, the teacher is to follow that lead and find additional resources so that they may immerse themselves in the topic.

Creating Your Own Unique Philosophy

If you are anything like me, elements of each of these resonate. However, many other factors come into play when creating your own educational philosophy. The type of early childhood experiences you have had will influence your thoughts. If you have worked in a classroom, those encounters color your perception of the teacher's role. Perhaps you have your own children and what they need adds yet another layer to your perfect educational dream.

To solidify your ideas about what early childhood education should be, ponder the following questions and write down your responses. Be brave! Be confident! Be you!

- What is a teacher's role in an early childhood classroom?
- How structured should a child's day be?
- How much free play versus teacher-directed activity should there be?
- What is the purpose of early childhood education for the child?
- What is the purpose of early childhood education for the family?
- What is the purpose of early childhood education for society?

Branch Out

Now take all of your answers and pull them together in a sentence or two that clearly defines what you think about early child-hood education.

You are ready to share your vision with your community.

CHAPTER 2

What Makes a Childcare Professional?

"Once you realize that you're in something that you've always wanted and you don't want to lose it, you behave differently. And that means integrity, professionalism, and knowing what's right from wrong and still making choices that you probably shouldn't have made." – Paul Anka, singer/ songwriter/ actor

When you start out as a director, it can be hard to be taken seriously. I know it was for me. You see, I started in this racket when I was just 23. Everyone was older than I was. I mean, *everyone*. Who would ever listen to me? But this was my dream. I had always wanted to run my own early childhood program. I just hadn't seen this challenge coming. This issue smacked me upside the head the first time I attended the convention for National Association for the Education of Young Children as a new director. I couldn't get the vendors to talk to me. I literally had thousands of dollars that I was planning to spend on equipment and materials at this huge convention, and no one would talk to me. Instead, I got a lot of "Send your director or owner over, and we'll give them a price list. Here, have a pen." How infuriating!

What Makes a Childcare Professional?

I *was* the director and owner. It was *my* money. I had saved every penny for years to make my dream come true. But because I went to the conference in casual clothes and I was obviously young, I wasn't seen as a professional. I learned a painful lesson that day. Hopefully you will learn from my pain and recognize the value of presenting yourself as the professional director you are.

Also, both professional and unprofessional behavior color all activities of a program. If we want our programs to be seen as professional, high-quality, and successful, it's up to us to set the stage. As their leaders and managers, the parents and staff look to us for cues. If we hold up high standards of professional conduct, our programs will follow. If we are half-hearted, they will follow that, too. It's good to remember that our first job is that of role model. Model well. It will make all the difference in the end.

By definition, a childcare professional is someone who provides quality care for children and their families. She implements the best practices she knows and continually increases her knowledge base. As such, this person would:

- Dress appropriately and strategically for her program
- Represent herself and her program thoughtfully, in person as well as in her email, website, and social media outlets

Behave ethically, resourcefully, and actively within her community Basically, she has her Big Girl Pants on all the time.

If we want to be seen as a professionals—and perhaps more importantly, to see ourselves as professionals—we will learn how to constantly carry ourselves in a professional manner. This is a unique challenge for us in the childcare industry since our field does not typically demand that we dress in business clothes and carry briefcases. Nevertheless, as directors we have this awesome privilege and responsibility of setting the tone for our teachers. They start to see themselves as professionals when we start to communicate the importance of the work they do: helping to better shape these small humans' self-confidence and perceptions of the world, mirroring how to better solve problems and manage their emotions, and ultimately teaching them how to make better choices in both the short- and long-term. Basically, we know exactly how much of a very, very big deal all of this really is. So now let's turn our attention to what conveys these messages most powerfully and memorably.

Let's Talk Clothes

Yes, this is your permission to shop! Pre-plan your wardrobe for easy mornings and professional presentation, and you'll thank yourself later. Here is what I found worked for me:

Find three pairs of slacks and two skirts in your two favorite colors to wear. For bonus points, ladies, get one simple dress, too. Then find ten tops that work with those two colors, some plain and some patterned. At least two of them should have your company logo on them.

Add a jacket or two. How dressy or casual they should be, will be based on your center's culture, but a good rule of thumb is one or two steps more formal than your teachers' dress code. Choose shoes that will allow you to adapt to any situation in your center. You never know when you might have to step into a classroom or take over the playground. You do know that you'll be on your feet a lot most days, so comfort needs to be a high priority. Keep a pair of super-cute shoes tucked away in your desk for impromptu visits or special occasions, but for the day-to-day a good pair of loafers or flats is definitely your friend. Now you don't have to spend mental energy on deciding what to wear. Save that for your job.

Focusing on What Matters

What matters may not be necessarily be what is most important. In the grand scheme of things, who you are is much more important than how you present yourself. But does how you present yourself matter? I mean, does it have an impact? Is it a factor that others consider when making assessments and decisions? Most definitely yes.

- Now let's make sure your interpersonal style matches your new professional look. *Your body language matters.* It's okay to practice the basics like how to give a firm handshake, how to maintain good eye contact, and how to flash a genuine smile. Do this, and families and staff actually feel your confidence.
- *Your choice of words matters.* Be mindful of using professional language when you conduct parent conferences, handle staff conflicts, and even explain commonplace events at your center. This could be the difference between informing a parent that "Timmy had a toileting accident today" and just blurting out "Timmy peed in his pants at naptime." If this kind of language is not already common in your center, it may be a golden opportunity to hold an in-service training and have it count as staff-wide professional hours.
- *How you deliver your words matter.* Do you know that your smile even comes through on the phone? So, get really good at explaining your educational philosophy with enthusiasm. This is your winning monologue, so definitely commit it to memory. In fact, if you can swing it, working on your telephone and in-person voice with an acting coach or professional speaker is a great use of an evening. Just make sure you have them sign a homemade training certificate to count for your professional development hours.
- *How you allow your staff to dress matters.* Bottom line—Cutoffs and tank tops just won't cut it. They need to be dressed professionally, too. Depending on your clientele, this might mean khaki shorts and a branded t-shirt, or it might mean slacks and a blouse. In any case, parents need to be able to readily identify a teacher, helper, or substitute teacher in a classroom at pickup time. A solid rule to

follow is that you and administrative staff should be dressed one step more formally than the teachers.

- *When you come to work matters.* You can't go wrong by coming early to greet your staff. Cultivating this front-porch philosophy models how important it is for them to come early and greet their families. You might not have to do it every day, but you do need to do it often enough to see the positive effects.
- *Your helpfulness and availability matter.* Be prepared to humble yourself and fill in where you're needed, whether it's changing diapers or pouring the snack-time juice. No job should be too small. A gentle reminder for those of us who love our nails: paint them, pretty them, but don't allow them to impede your doing any job in your center. If teachers or parents notice your hesitancy, it could give the wrong impression.
- *Your playfulness matters.* This job is about creating a joyful place to learn, so take time out each week to just go enjoy the wonder of being a child. For me, sliding down the slide at least once a week keeps me tuned into why I do this.
- *Your self-care matters.* It is super easy to get run down in this industry, so please eat real food and drink lots of water. Also, watching your way-of-eating and getting some exercise helps keep you from catching every little germ that floats in the front door.

Last but certainly not least, build some Snuggle Time into your to-do list. No lawyer or computer programmer gets the kind of perks we do. Spend time in classes on the floor with the children, and you'll get yourself some pretty awesome hugs.

Keys to Professionalism in Early Education

These are considered benchmarks or non-negotiables within our industry. They are expected, they are valued, and they are trustworthy.

- *Confidentiality:* Both director and staff must use the utmost discretion with these three types of information, making reasonable efforts to protect a family's privacy:
  - Family status
  - Financial information
  - Medical and developmental issues

- *Consistency:* Make a point of asking yourself these questions often:
  - "Does this behavior reflect what is in my documents?"
  - "Did I do this same behavior last week?"
  - "If I continue in this behavior, is this how I want to be remembered?"
- *Education:* Continue to develop professionally through workshops, educational seminars, or college courses. Through their conferences and conventions, organizations like NAEYC provide excellent educational and team-building opportunities throughout the year.
- *Ethical Conduct:* If you have questions on what is right or wrong in a specific situation, review one of the ethical codes of conduct from educational professional organizations. More on that coming up.
- *Resourcefulness:* Have an active resource file, appropriate resource directories, and an active network of contacts both inside and outside your field.
- *Honesty:* Convey the facts to your clients. Keep your staff up to date about issues. Be accurate in paperwork.
- *Alertness:* Know your staff and your parents. Perform spot observations. Read pertinent periodicals.
- *Mindfulness:* You are a model to the community, your staff, the children in your care, and their parents. Relationships between staff and parents must maintain a professional distance.

You know the culture and climate of your program best, so some of these will be more important for you to focus on than others. So, ask yourself:

- At this point in my career, which keys are most important to me right now?
- At this point in my staff's development, which keys might require more attention or training? What would be the best methods to increase the professionalism of my staff in these areas of greatest concern?

Keeping these keys in mind will make your center run smoothly. Stress the importance of them to your staff at meetings & trainings to keep them up to your standards. One way to do this is to adopt an ethical code for your program.

Ethics

Honesty, confidentiality, fairness, and respect, these terms can certainly be vague. What does that mean for your center? How do we know what's acceptable and what isn't from one day to the next? Enter the ethics statement, otherwise known as your center's code of conduct. Since formal regulations typically represent only a base requirement for care, quality programs don't just follow regulations; they exceed them. Providers should choose to make them that way. Their ethics demand it. Your program's ethics statement or code of conduct should be written down clearly and reviewed occasionally with all staff members. If you do choose to create your own, I encourage you to do this cooperatively with the other members of your team. It is a great community-building activity. Together you can craft detailed statements that describe behaviors associated with the ethics that your center wants to uphold.

For additional inspiration, organizations such as the National Association of Child Care Professionals have created their own codes of conduct. Below is the NACCP's Code of Conduct from which you may borrow, expound, adapt, or adopt:

1. To maintain the ethical standards of the National Association of Child Care Professionals to more effectively serve our children, their parents, and the field.

2. To continually remember that ours is a service industry. We are committed to providing quality childcare to our children and their families, and we place this service above personal gain.
3. To conduct our business in a way that will both maintain goodwill within the field and build the confidence of parents, the community, and fellow professionals.
4. To cooperatively work with parents and faithfully deliver the kind of service promised to them, whether orally, in writing, or implied.
5. To charge a fair tuition that will enable us to pay a fair living wage to the director and staff at our centers.
6. To maintain the appropriate child-to-staff ratios that will ensure provision of quality service to our children and their families.
7. To hire qualified individuals and to train them to work within the guidelines of this code of ethics.
8. To avoid sowing discontent among the employees of competitors with the purpose of embarrassing or hindering their business.
9. To avoid possible damage to a competitor's image by purposefully misleading parents, members of the community, or fellow professionals.
10. To support the policies and programs of our Association and to participate in its regional and national activities.
11. To conduct ourselves at all times in a way that will bring credit to our Association and the childcare field.

For the NAEYC code of conduct visit http://www.naeyc.org/store/node/450.

Distance

The last element to address is professional distance, maintaining an understood separation from both your staff and the families you serve. Yes, you want to care for them, empathize with them, and support them, but not to the point of becoming entangled with them emotionally. That just isn't professional. Yes, this job can feel lonely at times, so it is tempting to see your employees as your friends, as comrades-in-arms. But not only is it inappropriate, but it also makes it downright awkward and practically impossible to be impartial when something goes wrong.

For example, a center that I was consulting with almost lost its license because the owner and the director were close friends. Let's call the owner Fran and the director Judith. The center had three different serious violations, which led Licensing to start termination procedures to officially close the center. But each time something happened, Judith always provided Fran with an excuse and addressed the issue—sort of. Even when an assistant put a child at risk, Judith only talked to the employee and moved her to another room instead of firing her outright or at least retraining her. Every incident was similar. Judith did the barest minimum to get by. That is, until the week when Judith went on vacation and Fran stepped in for her. While doing scheduled file checks, Fran discovered that absolutely nothing had been updated in almost a year. Yes, Judith is clearly at fault. However, Fran wasn't supervising as closely as she should have or would have with any other employee because Judith was her friend. If your employees become your friends, odds are that this can and will happen. You have to create some distance.

If you were promoted from within the center, this is especially difficult. These were your peers, and now they are your subordinates. This means you cannot go out for drinks together anymore. You can socialize, just in a different way. Imagine the office parties you've seen in movies. The good boss is clearly not behaving the same way as everyone else.

So, how do you avoid feeling lonely? You find or create a peer group of other directors or small business leaders. A mastermind or networking group is ideal. You need to have folks who understand and sympathize with the same problems you are facing. Personally and professionally, it's worth the effort.

Branch Out

Which of the keys to professionalism will be most important to you?

CHAPTER 3

How Do I Get the Most Out of My Center?

"A goal without a deadline is just a dream."
– Robert Herjavec, businessman & investor

Once upon a time there was a little girl named Carrie, and she had her favorite place. That place was the classroom, *her* classroom. She loved the way that the teachers took care of her and taught her amazing things. Like why a cirrus cloud looks that way and how it was different from the puffy, cotton-ball clouds called cumulonimbus. Who knew that such things even had names? She decided that when she grew up, she would have a school like this of her own where children got to play and learn and sit in awe of teachers who read stories with sound effects and distinctive voices for every character. One day she would own her own school, a school for young children.

From the time I was four years old, I knew that I was going to grow up and run my own childcare center or, as we know call them frequently, early learning centers. It was the only dream I ever had. I held down two or three jobs at a time from the time I was old enough to work, saving up all I could to fuel that dream.

One of those jobs was at one of the best childcare programs in my area, which only took care of children until they turned two. It was a good place for me to grow as an educator for a little while. Then I got married and had my first child. Knowing how this game is played, I immediately got on waiting list at lots of programs in the hope that one of them would have room for my daughter when she turned two.

I never heard back from any of those centers.

It became obvious that I needed to do something because my child would soon become too old to attend my center and we had no place for her to go. We needed another option, so right then and there, the best option became opening my own center. My dream had a deadline. I needed to open my center before my daughter turned two. I knew the steps and had been working on them for years. I had supplies and equipment already stockpiled. I had lesson plans already written. I had already interviewed realtors and been scouting for properties. Now it was time to take the final steps: find a location, acquire it, do the necessary renovations, and get my license. Goal accomplished!

Staying on Track: What Are We Doing and Why?

Goal setting is arguably the single most important aspect in growing both personally and professionally. Usually, the daily events in a busy early childhood program dictate how our time and energy are spent. When this happens, faraway dreams and ambiguous plans are often pushed to the back of the priority list. But having clear, workable goals mapped out ahead of time gives your program structure and propels those plans forward.

I have heard from many people over the years that they aren't goal setters. If this tape is running in your mind right now, I want to offer you a different perspective. When you see the word "goal," think "problem solution." I had a problem: my daughter needed a quality school to attend, and there wasn't a place for her. My husband and I solved the problem by opening our center at bit earlier than planned. It is just a matter of perspective.

Specific goals are achieved through specific actions. The methods that are successful in achieving accreditation may not be the same as those necessary for modifying and enriching your curriculum or increasing your family involvement. Let's look at some specific goals and see how you might most effectively achieve each one.

Identifying Your Targets

The first step is to set aside time to set your goals and solve your problems. In fact, take advantage of milestones in your life or business and use them as fuel to set new goals. These may include job changes, mate changes, address changes, changes of seasons, anniversaries, or even birthdays. The most common time to set goals may be New Year's Eve, but don't be common. Be yourself.

You don't have to set goals in all areas of your business. That can be overwhelming. Narrowing it down to one or two areas gives you a much better chance at success. Here is a list of the areas of business growth that we suggest you explore.

The Seven Basic Business Goal Areas

1. Environmental
2. Staff development
3. Client
4. Community
5. Financial
6. Advocacy
7. Business plan

First, decide if you want to make changes quickly or over time. *Short-term goals* are things you want to change or accomplish within the next six months. For example, replacing your center's front door with one with an individualized key code for each family would be a reasonable short-term business goal. Of course, *long-term goals* are those that take longer than six months to achieve. If you are considering at a goal that you know will take more than two years, I suggest breaking it into smaller long-term goals.

Once you have the pinpointed the area and the necessary time frame, it is time to open the floodgates! There are no wrong answers or stupid ideas in brainstorming. Sometimes it starts out with a steady flow of ideas, and at other times it is like pulling teeth... slow and painful. That's normal. Just work on it until you have at least five possible ways to address the area you selected. Don't worry if you end up with a list of 20—That works, too. Some areas just tend to be more fertile. For example, you may be bursting at the seams with ideas to change the center's environment like new equipment, new choices of paint, or new usage of rooms while only being able to come up with a handful of ways to improve in your center's financial situation. There's no judgment in brainstorming.

- When the flow of ideas has slowed, take a moment to marvel at all the possible futures. Understandably, you can't do all of these ideas all at once. Some will have to be put aside, and some will happen in the future. Go through and evaluate which one's appeal to you the most and best meet your immediate needs. Generally, two or three rise to the top pretty quickly. These are your Divisional Champions. They now advance to the finals, where risks and benefits are weighed carefully before the grand goal is selected. Take your time with this part. Give each one a lot of thought and look at it from many angles. Consider these questions:
- *What are the potential risks? What are the potential positives? Who might get in your way or be hurt by this option? Who might be able to work with you to accomplish this? What problems might it solve in other areas?* With all the positives and negatives laid out, it is time to make a decision. Once it is selected, commit to it. Don't waffle.
- You now have your winner, so let's start training! This involves identifying the steps needed to achieve this particular goal. For example, if my goal is to increase enrollment by ten full-time children, what steps will accomplish this? First, determine where I

can accept enrollment. Which classrooms already have openings or room to increase class size? Another possibility is converting a multipurpose room into an active classroom. What needs to be done to make those classrooms more marketable? Next, develop a marketing strategy and budget for this room or rooms. Set mini-goals of number of tours or enrollment conversations. Who might I need to reach out to for assistance with this?

Remember, a goal without a deadline is just a dream. If timelines are too stringent, any goal can grow quickly out of reach. If they are too lenient, you risk losing focus. You need to have a challenge.

A highly challenging goal is best broken into several doable sub-goals. As you achieve each sub-goal, your subconscious works on your behalf and helps propel you to the next. By setting and reaching goals often, your subconscious eventually accepts this as the status quo.

Also, affiliating with others who are like-minded opens up a world of possibilities and accelerates your goal progress. It definitely helps if:

- Those with whom you affiliate are seeking the same thing as you, at the same time and with the same intensity. If they are located nearby, all the better.
- Small teams and one-to-one partnerships can spur you on to heights you simply cannot achieve on your own.
- Synergy is when one plus one equals more than two. Forging partnerships and affiliations make synergy possible.

Be forewarned… Even though on a conscious level you might truly want to change, your subconscious may conclude that you want to stay right where you are. The good news is that your subconscious is no match for the ability to master powerful, life-enhancing positive thoughts, so create affirmations that motivate and support you and read them out loud. You can't afford to use negative language or to harbor negative thoughts if you intend to make swift progress toward positive goals. What is the difference between a goal and a dream? Committing it to paper and setting a deadline.

You need some quiet time to reflect on the goals you've set and the goals you'd like to set. No one does his or her best thinking amid clamor and commotion.

When putting your goals on paper, you have many options including simply listing them or creating one of a variety of charts. Pursue only a few goals at a time and keep things as simple as possible.

Make a commitment to yourself and to your team to execute. Set a deadline. Change will not happen without commitment. Change is tough, but you are tougher!

Still Searching for a Worthy Goal? Explore These!

Accreditation

Accreditation involves voluntarily meeting higher quality standards. Agencies such NAEYC (National Association for the Education of Young Children), and NECPA (National Early Childhood Program Accreditation), both offer national accreditation. In addition, your state Child Care Block Grant (CCBG) funder probably has an accreditation system, and achieving this status increases your revenue from the CCBG agency. In Texas it is called Texas Rising Star. But be warned: non-governmental accreditations will have fees associated with them. Any way you slice it, accreditation is both a marketing tool and a practical, effective way to raise your center's commitment to professionalism.

This is an exciting and time-intensive goal, and it can feel like a never-ending process. Therefore, both staff and parents should recognize and be proud of the gradual progress of each teacher and classroom. For example, plan mini-celebrations when different phases of the process are completed. This can be an actual party, a well-deserved round of applause, public recognition of the people who encouraged or pushed the hardest, or a bulletin board marking the center's overall progress. Other occasions to celebrate may include:

- Completing their classroom observations
- Enacting the desired environmental or interaction improvements

- Completing all of the staff and parent surveys Discussing and agreeing on the final classroom ratings with the director
- Requesting the final accreditation visit Receiving the final accreditation... finally!

Each stage is a small victory in the process of achieving this larger goal. The options are endless.

Creating a New Professional Development Program

Start by involving those who will benefit the most and find out who would like to be part of the committee to plan the program. Ask them the following: *What* do you want to learn?

How would you like to learn: a class, a conference, online, reading articles?

When can you make the time: during naptime, at a staff meeting, in the evenings, on weekends?

Who would you like to see as the teacher: the director, a colleague, the licensing rep?

Re-energizing Training and Development

This is different from the previous goal. Here you will be building on a policy or a process that you already have developed. Move toward this goal by identifying one or two staff members who have not taken advantage of your staff training and development program. Ask for their help in rethinking your training system and requirements. They may be skeptical at first, but assure them that you need real, honest feedback. Ask why the program you have in place is not being utilized and how you could all work together to make it more engaging. Listen carefully and create a plan to follow their suggestions.

Working on the School Improvement Plan

This may be a single or multi-year project. Tackle each part of the goal or plan and break it into smaller segments. Find a colleague from another program who is working on a similar project and suggest you help each other as accountability partners. If you both need help on a particular topic, go to another source in the school or district and ask for assistance. Agree on checkpoints and monitor each other's progress. Celebrate when one of you meets a target; you will motivate each other!

Improving Family Participation

Begin with one or two interested and involved family members and ask for their ideas, suggestions and help in gaining the support of others. Consider involving the individual who questions or wants to discuss everything about the program. Ask them to be the chair or to serve on the executive committee of your parent support group. Channeling this energy and concern in a positive direction can be very exciting and productive.

Key Rules For Goal Setting

- *Goals set for you by others won't work.*
- *Never tamper with a set goal.*
- *A goal is an end in itself.*
- *You have to go public with your goal.*
- *All progress is good.*
- *Chip away at your goal a little at a time.*

Branch Out

Take the time to really think about what you really want in one area of your life and set a goal. Go through the steps:

- *Identify the area of the goal*
- *Is it short-term or long term?* • *Brainstorm!*
- *Pick the two or three best options*
- *Weigh the risks and benefits* • *Select a winner!*
- *Determine sub-goals and deadlines*
- *Think through needed resources*
- *Write it down and commit!*

CHAPTER 4

How Do I Talk and Write Effectively?

"What we've got here is a failure to communicate." – Frank Pierson

Early on in my career, I had a situation where communication had the chance to make or break my relationship with a client. This client was the father of a toddler, a toddler who had bitten other children and had been bitten herself... as toddlers are wont to do. But the third time it happened, Dad got upset. When he talked to the teacher in the classroom, she replied that toddlers are prone to inappropriately use their teeth: some use them on other children, some on themselves, others on inanimate objects. It is a normal part of their development. Still, Dad wanted to know the protocol: so, what happens when a child bites? Do the child's parents get notified? Is the child removed from the program? Is there any disciplinary action?

The teacher then informed him of our policy: immediately address the biting with both children using developmentally appropriate redirection and behavior management; later on, inform the parent of the bitten child of the incident since first aid was rendered. Dad was confused. "You mean the parents of the child who bites don't even know that their child is biting other kids?" "No," the teacher answered. "There's no need for the parents to know because the situation was handled in the classroom at that time. These issues generally resolve themselves." With that, the teacher assumed the issue was resolved. For Dad, however, it was far from over. In fact, he was positively livid. He stormed into my office and demanded a meeting, so one was scheduled.

In the meeting he wanted to know how we could ethically make the decision to—in his exact words—"hide the truth from parents." In order to not have any secrets kept from him, his solution was that the teacher calls him every time his child shows aggression toward another child, including every time she bit or hit or pinched or pulled hair or pushed someone down. Every. Time. Practically, the teacher knew she would not be able to comply with what he wanted. Moreover, she knew it would change the way she thought about this child. She would be constantly forced to focus on the negative behaviors, ignoring all of this child's wonderful qualities. The teacher wanted to continue addressing issues as they arose, offering to tell Dad if his child seemed to become a habitual biter.

At this point, neither of the parties could see where the other one was coming from. It took a lot of time, a lot of open and honest communication, and a willingness to actively listen and to put ourselves in the other's shoes, but we all got to a place of understanding and came up with a plan that worked for everyone. It was worth it.

In the end Dad became one of our school's loudest cheerleaders, actively recruiting new families and staying enrolled until his daughter left for kindergarten.

Can't stress this enough… Establishing good communication with staff and clients is the hard work necessary to ensure that your program continues to run smoothly and profitably.

Identifying Communication Styles

Since effective communication skills require a high level of self-awareness, understanding personal styles of communicating will go a long way toward helping to create good and lasting impressions on others. By becoming more aware of how others perceive us, we can adapt more readily to their styles of communicating. Now this does not mean that we have to be chameleons, changing with every personality we meet. It's more about making the effort to help other people feel more comfortable with us and to recognize how we may more readily understand them. So let's examine traditional communication styles. Discovering which style best fits you can be done in a number of ways including personality tests such as the Myers-Briggs Type Indicator® (MBTI®) instrument, psychological assessments, and self-assessments. There are countless different systems for classifying personality types, and each lends some clarity to how you interact with the world. It is a useful element of self-discovery.

When it comes to communication styles, take a look at the characteristics of the three main communication styles and see which one you use most. Are you aggressive, passive, or assertive?

Elements of the Aggressive Style

- Mottos and Beliefs "Everyone should be like me." "I am never wrong." "I've got rights, but you don't."
- Communication Style Closed-minded Poor listener Has difficulty seeing the other person's point of view Interrupts Monopolizes the conversation
- Characteristics Achieves goals, often at others' expense Domineering, bullying Patronizing Condescending, sarcastic
- Behavior Puts others down Doesn't ever think they are wrong Bossy Moves into people's space, overpowers Jumps on others, pushes people around Know-it-all attitude Doesn't show appreciation
- Nonverbal Cues Points, shakes finger Frowns Squints eyes critically Glares Stares Rigid posture Critical, loud, yelling tone of voice Fast, clipped speech
- Verbal Cues "You must, you should, you ought, you better…" "Don't ask why. Just do it." Confrontation and Problem Solving Must win arguments, threatens, attacks Operates from win/lose position
- Feelings Felt Anger Hostility Frustration Impatience

Effects Provokes counter-aggression, alienation from others, ill health Wastes time and energy over supervising others Pays high price in human relationships Fosters resistance, defiance, sabotaging, striking back, forming alliances, lying, covering up Forces compliance with resentment

Elements of the Passive Style

- Mottos and Beliefs "Don't express your true feelings." "Don't make waves." "Don't disagree." "Others have more rights than I do."
- Communication Style Indirect Always agrees Doesn't speak up Hesitant
- Characteristics Apologetic, self-conscious Trusts others, but not self Doesn't express own wants and feelings Allows others to make decisions for self Doesn't get what he or she wants
- Behaviors Sighs a lot Tries to sit on both sides of the fence to avoid conflict Clams up when feeling treated unfairly Asks permission unnecessarily Complains instead of taking action Lets others make choices Has difficulty implementing plans Self-effacing
- Nonverbal Cues Fidgets Nods head often; comes across as pleading Lack of facial animation Smiles and nods in agreement Downcast eyes Slumped posture Low volume, meek Up talk Fast when anxious, slow/hesitant when doubtful
- Verbal Cues "You should do it." "You have more experience than I do." "I can't..." "This is probably wrong, but..." "I'll try..." Monotone, low energy
- Confrontation and Problem Solving Avoids, ignores, leaves, postpones Withdraws, is sullen and silent Agrees externally, while disagreeing internally Expends energy to avoid conflicts that are anxiety provoking Spends too much time asking for advice, supervision Agrees too often
- Feelings Felt Powerlessness Wonders why doesn't receive credit for good work Chalks up lack of recognition to others' inabilities

Effects: Gives up being him/herself Builds dependency relationships Doesn't know where he or she stands Slowly loses self-esteem Promotes other's causes Is not well-liked

Elements of the Assertive Style

- Mottos and Beliefs Believes self and others are valuable Knowing that assertiveness doesn't mean you always win, but that you handled the situation as effectively as possible "I have rights and so do others."
- Communication Style Effective, active listener States limits, expectations States observations, no labels or judgments Expresses self directly, honestly, and as soon as possible about feelings and wants Checks on other's feelings
- Characteristics Non-judgmental Observes behavior rather than labeling it Trusts self and others Confident Self-aware Open, flexible, versatile Playful, sense of humor Decisive Proactive, initiating
- Behavior Operates from choice Knows what is needed and develops a plan to get it Action-oriented Firm Realistic expectations Fair, just Consistent Takes appropriate action toward getting what you want without denying rights of others
- Nonverbal Cues Open, natural gestures Attentive, interested facial expression Direct eye contact Confident or relaxed posture Vocal volume appropriate, expressive Varied rate of speech
- Verbal Cues "I choose to..." "What are my options?" "What alternatives do we have?"
- Confrontation and Problem Solving Negotiates, bargains, trades off, compromises Confronts problems at the time they happen Doesn't let negative feelings build up
- Feelings Felt Enthusiasm Well-being Even tempered

Effects: Increased self-esteem and self-confidence Increased self-esteem of others Feels motivated and understood Others know where they stand Keep in mind that very few people are all one style. While the assertive style is usually the one to strive for, the style has to match the situation. For example, the aggressive style becomes essential when decisions have to be made quickly during emergencies. Passiveness also has its critical applications, especially when an issue is minor or when the problems caused by the conflict might become greater than the conflict itself. If emotions are running high, then it makes sense to take a break in order to calm down and regain perspective.

Remaining aware of your own communication style and fine-tuning it as time goes by gives you the best chance of success in business and life.

The Power of Effective Listening

Once you have looked at your speaking style it is time to turn your attention to listening. To improve listening skills, consider the following:

POOR LISTENER	EFFECTIVE LISTENER
Tends to space out with slow speakers.	Thinks and mentally summarizes, weighs the evidence, listens between the lines to tones of voice and evidence
Tunes out speaker when subject is dry	Finds what is in it for me
Easily distracted	Fights distractions, sees past bad communication habits and knows how to concentrate
Takes intensive notes, but the more notes taken, the less value; has only one way to take notes	Has two-to-three ways to take notes and organize important information
Is over-stimulated, tends to seek and enter into arguments	Does not judge until comprehension is complete
Inexperienced in listening to difficult material; has usually sought light, recreational materials	Uses "heavier" materials to regularly exercise the mind.
Lets colorful words catch his or her attention	Interprets colorful language and doesn't get hung up on it
Shows no energy output	Holds eye contact and helps speaker along by showing an active body state
Judges delivery, tunes out	Judges content, skips over delivery errors
Listens for facts	Listens for central ideas

It is not only what you say in the classroom that is important, but how you say it can make the difference to students. Nonverbal messages are an essential component of communication in the teaching process. Teachers should be aware of nonverbal behavior in the classroom for three major reasons: An awareness of nonverbal behavior will allow you to become better receivers of students' messages. You will become a better sender of signals that reinforce learning. This mode of communication increases the degree of the perceived psychological closeness between teacher and student. Some major areas of nonverbal behaviors to explore are: Eye contact Facial expressions Gestures Posture and body orientation Proximity Para linguistics Humor

Eye contact

Eye contact, an important channel of interpersonal communication, helps regulate the flow of communication. It signals interest in others. Furthermore, eye contact with audiences increases the speaker's credibility. Teachers who make eye contact open the flow of communication and convey interest, concern, warmth, and credibility.

Facial expressions

Smiling is a powerful cue that transmits: Happiness Friendliness Warmth Liking Affiliation Thus, if you smile frequently, you will be perceived as more likable, friendly, warm, and approachable. Smiling is often contagious, and students will react favorably and learn more.

Gestures

If you fail to gesture while speaking, you may be perceived as boring, stiff, and unanimated. A lively and animated teaching style captures students' attention, makes the material more interesting, facilitates learning, and provides a bit of entertainment. Head nods, a form of gesture, communicate positive reinforcement to students and indicate that you are listening.

Posture and body orientation

You communicate numerous messages by the way you walk, talk, stand, and sit. Standing erect but not rigid and leaning slightly forward communicate to students that you are approachable, receptive, and friendly. Furthermore, interpersonal closeness results when you and your students face each other. Speaking with your back turned or looking at the floor or ceiling should be avoided; it communicates disinterest to your class.

Proximity

Cultural norms dictate a comfortable distance for interaction with students. You should look for signals of discomfort caused by invading students' space. Some of these are: Rocking Leg swinging Tapping Gaze aversion Typically, in large classes, space invasion is not a problem. In fact, there is usually too much distance. To counteract this, move around the classroom to increase interaction with your students. Increasing proximity enables you to make better eye contact and increases the opportunities for students to speak.

Para linguistics

This facet of nonverbal communication includes such vocal elements as: Tone Pitch Rhythm Timbre Loudness Inflection For maximum teaching effectiveness, learn to vary these six elements of your voice. One of the major criticisms is of instructors who speak in a monotone. Listeners perceive these instructors as boring and dull. Students report that they learn less and lose interest more quickly when listening to teachers who have not learned to modulate their voices.

Humor

Humor is often overlooked as a teaching tool, and it is too often not encouraged in classrooms. Laughter releases stress and tension for both instructor and student. You should develop the ability to laugh at yourself and encourage students to do the same. It fosters a friendly classroom environment that facilitates learning. Former NFL coach Lou Holtz wrote that when his players felt successful, he always observed the presence of good humor in the locker room. Obviously, adequate knowledge of the subject matter is crucial to your success; however, it's not the only crucial element. Creating a climate that facilitates learning and retention demands good nonverbal and verbal skills. To improve your nonverbal skills, record yourself speaking. Then ask a colleague in communications to suggest refinements.

By Vicki Ritts, St. Louis Community College at Florissant Valley and James R. Stein, Southern Illinois University, Edwardsville. (Reprinted by permission) As we discussed in the professionalism and marketing chapters, how you present your center will impact how parents feel about you. To a large degree, how you position your center will determine who calls your program for information and who comes in to look around. When parents or potential clients call or email, spend time with them. The longer you work with them the more insight you will gain into their needs, your customer profile, and additional services you could offer to improve your profitability. Then they are more likely to take the next step.

Take Notes on Phone Calls

From one five-minute phone call, you can collect contact information, demographics, concerns, hours of care they need, and so much other useful information. Document, document, document! These notes should be in one central location. I like to use an inbound communication log <insert website link>

Changing callers into prospects consistently takes follow-up and follow-through. Follow-up means getting back in touch with them. That is one of the great things about the communication log; it has a daily follow-up section and a weekly follow-up section. Follow-through means doing what you say you will. If you say you will call them back, *do it.* The more positive interactions you have with a family, the more likely they are to enroll at your center and refer other families to your program.

Once you have transformed the family from a caller to a prospect, it is time for the real work to begin. You need to have a message you repeat several times. This is called your tag line or your bumper sticker. Use the information you gained in your phone call or other contact to customize your presentation. Your tours will be somewhat scripted. There are things that you must cover with every perspective family. What those areas are will depend upon your center's strengths, and your policies. You will want to cover your hours, age groupings, and basic health policy.

After the tour you will need to follow up again. This can be a post card, thank-you note, or telephone call. Repeated contact will help move them from prospects to enrolled families.

Another venue for parent communication at many centers is the pre-enrollment interview or orientation. This is a chance for you to decide if the family is right for your program. Go through your policies in depth. This is also when the parent will tell you what their concerns are, what their skills are, how they can help you, and what their hopes are. This can be done individually or as a group orientation. How you handle enrollment sets the tone for their tenure with your program. Meet their needs to the best of your ability. You can schedule a weeklong transition, two days of transition, having them sit in on routines, allow them to drop in one day or have them start full-time the first day. There are pros and cons to each of these methods. Communication with established families is often over-looked. The parents need to hear from you early and often. Talk to them. Write to them. Message them on your communication app. Call them. Give them newsletters. Send them pictures of their child.

Tell them what is happening. Ask them questions.

You will have parents who are visual, kinetic, auditory, and tactile learners. You need to have a variety of ways to communicate with your client base to make sure you get your message out to all of them. Remember that the most successful communication has a goal behind it.

- Before you initiate communication, Determine your goal
- Craft a message
- Script your tag line
- Think about possible challenges
- Prepare responses
- Go do it!

Effective Communication Is Two-Way

- You need to listen to what they are saying. Active listening is key. Reflect back what they are saying: "*So, you are worried that Timmy won't do well in a class with mostly girls?*" Ask for clarification: "*I am unclear on what you are wanting on the menu? Are you asking for more raw foods?*"
- Express concern: "*I understand this is a rough time for your family.*"
- Take time: "*I am not sure, so let me look into that.*" "*Why don't you go on into my office. I just have to give Ms. Becky a message.*"
- Set up follow-up: "*Okay. I will talk to those people and get back to you on Friday.*"

When They Leave

When a family gives notice that they are leaving your center, visit with them. They are a fount of valuable information. Conduct an informal exit interview, send out a follow-up survey, or just call them on the phone. Find out what they think your center's strengths are. Find out why they are leaving. Find out what your biggest weakness is.

Ten Commandments of Parent Relations

1. The parent is never an interruption to your work.
2. Greet every parent with a friendly smile.
3. Call parents by name.
4. Remember that you and your employees are the company!
5. The parent is always right. Never argue with a parent.
6. Don't say, "I don't know."
7. Remember that the parent pays you and your staff.
8. Say it positively!
9. Brighten the parent's day.
10. Go the extra mile!

Branch Out

Create a communication plan for how you will handle inquiries, notify parents of upcoming field trips, handle late tuition, and announce a new teacher.

CHAPTER 5

Are These My Monkeys?

"Not my circus. Not my monkeys."– Polish saying

That saying is one of my favorites. I am constantly saying, *"Not my monkey"*... now. I used to be a monkey-chaser.

When I first opened my center, I wanted to make sure everyone knew that I was a caring and empathetic boss. I wanted my employees to know that I cared about them and wanted them at my center, that I would take good care of them. I had an employee who was probably about twice as old as I was. She had multiple children, the youngest of which was a teenager. One day she came into work, and she was just a mess. I mean, an emotional wreck. I asked her what was going on. She responded that she had the worst morning ever and proceeded to tell me this long, involved story about all kinds of teenage behavior. Basically, her son was being a twit and saying extremely rude things to his mother. I was concerned that this was borderline parental abuse. I just kept listening.

So, after she purged herself of all the horrors of the morning, I got her back to the point where she could work. I spent the rest of the morning looking for resources on how to parent this teenager. Since she already had three adult children, she had parented teenagers before and knew how to do it, but I thought that as her boss it was my job to go out and find resources for her. Since my eldest was only three and I didn't have personal experience to draw from, I had to seek everything out. I just didn't want to have another day when my employee was a complete wreck and couldn't work for the first half-hour of her shift.

So, I chased the monkey.

What I should have said after I had helped her to purge the poison was to ask, *"Do you need any help from me?"* If she said yes, then ask what help she needs. Only then should I have gone and gotten the resources. Otherwise, you are taking away her agency. Often people just need to vent. Set an expectation up front by giving a timeframe: *"I have fifteen minutes before I need to give Luke a break. Do you want to talk?"* That is the right way to manage a monkey like this.

Like I said, I did a lot early on. I wanted to be the good guy, so I chased down monkeys and treated them as my own, robbing others of the ability to fight their own battles and me of the ability to get my work done. I did it with their personal problems and their work.

For example, I would go out and get supplies that were mentioned in a teacher's lesson plan but not written on the supplies list. If I learned that they desperately needed the googly eyes or the special-shaped pasta or a pumpkin to carve or whatever, I would drop what I was doing and go get it for them. I would take care of their monkeys.

Now I'm constantly saying, *"Not my monkey."* I want you to know this power, too. Did you know that the average director makes it in this job for only 15 months? That is a ridiculous burnout rate, and the number-one reason is constantly taking care of someone else's monkeys. Learn to recognize them. Learn to manage them. But you absolutely cannot take care of other people's monkeys.

So, say it with me, right now, out loud: *"Not my circus, not my monkeys!"*

Management Time: Who's Got the Monkey?

By William Oncken, Jr., (former CEO, The William Oncken Company of Texas, Inc.) and Donald L. Wass (former President, The William Oncken Company of Texas, inc.)

Adapted from an article in the Harvard Business Review as an analogy that underscores the value of assigning, delegating and controlling.

In any organization the director's bosses, peers, clients, and staff–in return for their active support–impose some requirements; just as the director imposes some requirements upon them where they draw on his support. These demands constitute so much of the director's time that successful leadership hinges on an ability to control this "monkey-on-the-back" input effectively.

Why is it that directors are typically running out of time while their staff is typically running out of work? In this article, we shall explore the meaning of management time as it relates to the interaction between directors, their bosses, their own peers, and their staff. Specifically, we shall deal with three different kinds of management time:

Boss-imposed time – to accomplish those activities which the boss requires and which the director cannot disregard without direct and swift penalty.

System-imposed time – to accommodate those requests to the director for active support from his peers. This assistance must also be provided lest there be penalties, though not always direct or swift.

Self-imposed time – to do those things which the director originates or agrees to do. A certain portion of this kind of time, however, will be taken by staff and is called "staff-imposed time." The remaining portion will be your own and is called "discretionary time." Self-imposed time is not subject to penalty since neither the boss, nor the system can discipline the director for not doing what they did not know the director had intended to do in the first place.

The management of time necessitates that directors get control over the timing and content of what they do. Since what their bosses and the system impose on them are subject to penalty, directors cannot tamper with those requirements. Thus, their self-imposed time becomes their major area of concern.

Directors should try to increase the discretionary component of their self-imposed time by minimizing or doing away with the "staff" component. They will then use the added period of time to get better control over their boss-imposed and system-imposed activities. Most directors spend much more staff-imposed time than they even faintly realize. Hence, we shall use the analogy of a monkey-on-the-back to examine how staff-imposed time comes into being and what the superior can do about it.

Where Is the Monkey?

Let us imagine that a director is walking down the hall and then he notices one of his teachers, Jones, coming up the hallway. When they are abreast of one another, Jones greets the director with, *"Good morning. By the way, we've got a problem. You see..."* As Jones continues, the director recognizes in this problem the same two characteristics common to all the problems his staff gratuitously brings to his attention. Namely, the manger knows (a) enough to get involved, but (b) not enough to make the on-the-spot decision expected of him. Eventually, the director says, *"So glad you brought this up. I'm in a rush right now. Meanwhile, let me think about it and I'll let you know."* Then he and Jones part company.

Let us analyze what has just happened. Before the two of them met, on whose back was it? The teacher. Now whose back is it on? The director. Staff-imposed time begins the moment a monkey successfully executes a leap from the back of a staff member to the back of his superior, and it does not end until the monkey is returned to its proper owner for care and feeding.

In accepting the monkey, the director has voluntarily assumed a position subordinate to his staff. That is, he has allowed Jones to make him the subordinate by doing two things a subordinate is generally expected to do for a boss: the director has accepted a responsibility from his staff, and the director has promised a progress report.

The staff – to make sure the director does not miss this point – will later stick their head in the director's office and cheerily query, "How's it coming?" This is called "supervision."

Or let us imagine again, in concluding a working conference with another staff, Johnson, the director's parting words are *"Fine. Send me a memo on that."*

Let us analyze this one. The monkey is now on the staff's back because the next move is his, but it is poised for a leap. Watch that monkey. Johnson dutifully writes the requested memo and drops it in his out-basket. Shortly thereafter, the director plucks it from his in-basket and reads it. Whose move is it now? The director. If he does not make that move soon, he will get a follow-up memo from the staff. This is another form of supervision. The longer the director delays, the more frustrated the staff will become (he'll be "spinning his wheels"), and the guiltier the director will feel (his backlog of staff-imposed time will be mounting).

Or suppose once again that in a meeting with a third staff member, Smith, the director agrees to provide all the necessary backing for a fundraising campaign he has just asked Smith to develop. The director's parting words to her are *"Just let me know how I can help."*

Now let us analyze this. Here the monkey is initially on the staff's back, but for how long? Smith realizes that she cannot let the director "know" until her proposal has the director's approval. And from experience, she also realizes that her proposal will likely be sitting in the director's briefcase for weeks waiting for him to eventually get to it.

Whose really got the monkey? Who will be checking up on whom? Wheel spinning and bottlenecking are on their way again.

A fourth teacher, Reed, has just been transferred from another classroom in order to launch and eventually manage a newly created afterschool program. The director has said that they should get together soon to hammer out a set of objectives for the new job, and that *"I will draw up an initial draft for discussion with you."*

Let us analyze this one, too. The staff has the new job (by formal assignment) and the full responsibility (by formal delegation), but the director has the next move. Until he makes it, he will have the monkey and the staff will be immobilized.

Why does it all happen? Because in each instance the director and the staff assume at the outset, wittingly or unwittingly, that the matter under consideration is a joint problem. The monkey in each case begins its career astride both their backs. All it has to do now is move the wrong leg and presto! The staff deftly disappears. The director is thus left with another acquisition to his menagerie. Of course, monkeys can be trained not to move the wrong leg. But it is easier to prevent them from straddling backs in the first place.

Who Is Working for Whom?

To make what follows more credible, let us suppose that these same four staffers are so thoughtful and considerate of their superior's time that they are at pains to allow no more than three monkeys to leap from each of their backs to his in any one given day. In a five-day week, the director will have picked up 60 screaming monkeys, far too many to do anything about individually. So, he spends the staff-imposed time juggling his "priorities."

Late Friday afternoon, the director is in his office with the door closed for privacy in order to contemplate the situation while his staff is waiting outside to get a last chance before the weekend to remind him that he will have to "fish or cut bait." Imagine what they are saying to each other about the director as they wait: *"What a bottleneck." "He just can't make up his mind." "How anyone ever got that high up in our company without being able to make a decision, we'll never know."*

Worst of all, the reason the director cannot make any of these next moves is that his time is almost entirely eaten up in meeting his own boss-imposed and system-imposed requirements. To get control of these, he needs discretionary time that is in turn denied him when he is preoccupied with all these monkeys. The director is caught in a vicious cycle. But time is a-wasting (an understatement). The director calls his secretary on the intercom and instructs her to tell his staff that he will be unavailable to see them until Monday morning. At 7:00 pm., he drives home, intending with firm resolve to return to the office tomorrow to get caught up over the weekend. He returns bright and early the next day only to see, on the nearest green of the golf course across from his office window, a foursome. Guest who?

That does it. He now knows who is really working for whom. Moreover, he now sees that if he actually accomplishes during this weekend what he came to accomplish, his staff morale will go up so sharply that they will each raise the limit on the number of monkeys they will let jump from their backs to his. In short, he now sees – with the clarity of a revelation on a mountaintop – that the more he gets caught up, the more he will fall behind.

He leaves the office with the speed of a person running away from a plague. His plan? To get caught up on something else he hasn't had time for in years: a weekend with his family. This is one of the many varieties of discretionary time he has been denied. Sunday night he enjoys ten hours of sweet, untroubled slumber because he has clear cut plans for Monday. He is going to get rid of his staff-imposed time. In exchange, he will get an equal amount of discretionary time, part of which he will spend with his staff to see that they learn the difficult but regarding directorial art called "The Care and Feeding of Monkeys."

The director will also have plenty of discretionary time left over for getting control of the timing and content not only of his boss-imposed time but of his system-imposed time as well. All of this may take months, but compared with the way things have been, the rewards will be enormous. His ultimate objective is to manage his management time.

Getting Rid of the Monkeys

The director returns to the office Monday morning just late enough to permit his four staff to collect in his outer office wanting to see him about their monkeys. He calls them in, one by one. The purpose of each interview is to take a monkey, place it on the desk between them, and figure out together how the next move might conceivably be the staff's. For certain monkeys, this will take some doing. The staff's next move may be so elusive that the monkey sleeps on the staff's back overnight and have him or her return with it at an appointed time the next morning to continue the joint quest for a more substantive move by the staff. Monkeys sleep just as soundly overnight on the staff's backs as on the superiors'.

As each staff leaves the office, the director is rewarded by the sight of a monkey leaving his office on the staff's back. For the next 24 hours, the staff will not be waiting for the director. Instead, the director will be waiting for the staff.

Later, as if to remind himself that there is no law against his engaging in a constructive exercise in the interim, the director strolls by the staff's office, sticks his head in the door and cheerily ask, *"How's it coming?"* The time consumed in doing this is discretionary for the director and boss-imposed for the staff.

When the staff with the monkey on his or her back and the director meet at the appointed hour the next day, the director explains the ground rules in words to this effect:

"At no time while I am helping you with this or any other problem will your problem become my problem. The instant your problem becomes mine, you will no longer have a problem. I cannot help a person who hasn't got a problem.

"When this meeting is over, the problem will leave this office exactly the way it came in: on your back. You may ask my help at any appointed time, and we will make a joint determination of what the next move will be and which of us will make it.

"In those rare instances where the next move turns out to be mine, you and I will determine it together. I will not make any move alone."

The director follows this same line of thought with each staff until at about 11:00 am. He realizes that he has no need to shut his door. His monkeys are gone. They will return but by appointment only. His appointment calendar will assure this.

Transferring the Initiative

What we have been driving at with this monkey-on-the-back analogy is to transfer initiative from superior to staff and keep it there. We have tried to highlight a truism as obvious as it is subtle. Namely, before developing initiative in staff, the director must see to it that they have the initiative. Once he takes it back, they will no longer have it and the discretionary time can be kissed goodbye. It will all revert to staff-imposed time. Nor can both director and staff effectively have the same initiative at the same time. The opener, *"Boss, we've got a problem"* implies this duality and represents (as noted earlier) a monkey astride two backs, which is a very bad way to start a monkey on its career. Let us, therefore, take a few moments to examine what we prefer to call, "The Anatomy of Directorial Initiative." There are five degrees of initiative that the director can exercise in relation to the boss and to the system: (1) wait until told (lowest initiative), (2) ask what to do, (3) recommend, then take resulting action, (4) act but advise at once, and (5) act on own, then routinely report (highest initiative).

Clearly, the director should be professional enough not to indulge in Initiatives 1 and 2 in relation either to the boss or to the system. A director who uses Initiative 1 has no control over either the timing or content of boss-imposed or system-imposed time and thereby forfeits any right to complain about what he is told to do or when. The director who uses Initiative 2 has control over the timing but not over the content. Initiatives 3, 4 and 5 leave the director in control with the greatest control being at level 5.

The director's job – in relation to staff initiatives – is twofold: first, to outlaw the use of Initiatives 1 and 2, thus giving staff no choice but to learn and master "completed staff work;" second, see that for each problem leaving the office there is an agreed-upon level of initiative assigned to it, in addition to the agreed-upon time and place of the next director staff conference. The latter should be duly noted on the director's appointment calendar.

Care & Feeding of Monkeys

In order to further clarify our analogy between the monkey-on-the-back and the well-known processes of assigning and controlling, we shall refer briefly to the director's appointment schedule, which calls for five hard-and-fast rules governing the "Care and Feeding of Monkeys" (violations of these rules will cost discretionary time):

- *Rule 1*
  Monkeys should be fed or shot. Otherwise, they will starve to death and the director will waste valuable time on postmortems or attempted resurrections.
- *Rule 2*
  The monkey population should be kept below the maximum number the director has time to feed. Staff will find time to work as many

monkeys as he finds time to feed, but no more. It shouldn't take more than 5 to 15 minutes to feed a properly prepared monkey.

- *Rule 3*

  Monkeys should be fed by appointment only. The director should not have to be hunting down starving monkeys and feeding them on a catch-as-catch can basis.

- *Rule 4*

  Monkeys should be fed face to face or by telephone, but never by mail. If by mail, the next move will be the director's – remember? Documentation may add to the feeding process, but it cannot take the place of feeding.

- *Rule 5*

  Every monkey should have an assigned "next feeding time" and "degree of initiative." These may be revised at any time by mutual consent, but never allowed to become vague or indefinite. Otherwise, the monkey will either starve to death or wind up on the director's back.

Concluding Note

The first order of business is for the director to enlarge his discretionary time by eliminating staff-imposed time. The second is for the director to use a portion of this newfound discretionary time to see to it that each staff member possesses the initiative without which he cannot exercise initiative, and then to see to it that this initiative is in fact taken. The third is for the director to use another portion of the increased discretionary time to get and keep control of the timing and content of both boss-imposed and system-imposed time.

The result of all this is that the director's leverage will increase, in turn enabling the value of each hour spent in managing management time to multiply without theoretical limit.

Watch out for monkeys. The woods are full of them.

General Summary

The first rule of monkey management, that they should be fed of shot, is often the hardest one for people to get a handle on. Here is an example of shooting a monkey:

> Janice: *Can I have next Tuesday off?*
> Director: *Do you need an answer right now?*
> Janice: *Yes.*
> Director: *Then the answer is no.*

It is easy. I use this phrase all the time to execute monkeys. Try it the next time someone interrupts you with a monkey.

Another way to shoot a monkey is to ask if the person followed your procedure:

> Janice: *Can I have next Thursday off?*
> Director: *Did you fill out the day-off request two weeks before the date?*
> Janice: *No.*
> Director: *Then I cannot approve a substitute. You can see if you can find someone to cover for you and arrange coverage for your class. If you do, just put the room coverage form in the inbox.*

See? Not your monkey. It is Janice's. Creating systems for fending off monkeys like these is a key element of running a center without losing your mind. You need systems to create a monkey force field around you.

If you have decided to feed a monkey, that doesn't mean it has to stay your responsibility. You might simply be fostering the monkey until you can pass it off to a different caretaker: delegating the responsibility. Use delegation and take responsibility for your decisions and actions. Be aware that there is always a next move and that's where knowledge will allow you to be better prepared.

Branch Out

Practice shooting monkeys. Record how you feel and what happened.

CHAPTER 6

Who Can Get Things Done?

"In order to succeed, it's not the how or the what but who."
– Claudio Fernández-Aráoz

As a Director I left my center for two to three weeks every year. I'm not a mind-reader, but you are probably asking yourself, *"How in the world is that glorious possibility even remotely possible?"*

The answer is twofold. One element was officially closing my center for a week so that all of my staff got paid vacation. This way I didn't have to schedule individual vacations, and I didn't have to scramble for find substitutes. The other key element was delegation. I told my staff that while I was gone, I would check in once or twice a day (I started off with twice and moved to once after a few years) and gave them all my contact information. They could call me if a child or staff member went to the hospital in an ambulance or if there had been a fire or if someone had broken a law. Then I just enjoyed my vacation. I left town. I even left the state. I let the people whom I had trained run my center without me. Bear in mind that I did not do this my first year as a director because I had not yet created systems so that I could safely delegate. However, I made it a goal to do this as soon as I possibly could. Remember how goals need motivation? Well, I had it. I have a place that I love to go every summer, and it takes two days to drive there. If I only took the one week that I was closed, then I would only get four days at my favorite place. I needed more than a week in the summer, so I created systems to allow me to leave and know that the building would not catch on fire, that everybody would not dis-enroll, and that my staff would not quit. I needed a delegation plan, so I got pretty good at delegating.

The Process of Delegation

The process of delegation is straightforward. You just have to ask seven questions:

1. What are the elements of the task?
2. What are the abilities of the person to whom I want to delegate the task?
3. What are the resources available to do the task?
4. What outcomes are expected?
5. What date, time, or hour is the task due?
6. When are progress reports due?
7. When will you be available to consult on the task?

Once you have those answers you can assign the task to a person who is well-suited to it and then provide the needed support.

What is often the larger issue is determining what you should delegate. The last time I tried to write down all of the monthly activities a director does, I got to over 120 items. That is a lot to get done in 40 hours a week. Because of that, many directors work more hours in an attempt to get it all done. Which is why we burn out.

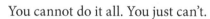

You cannot do it all. You just can't.

As they say in the song, "*Love is like a magic penny. Hold it tight and you won't have any. Lend it, spend it, give it away.*" The same is true for work. You already have so much it could be rolling all over the floor! Lend it out to others. It helps them and you.

Outsource some of it. That can mean eliminating unnecessary activities (*Do I really need to do those monthly employee file reviews?*), automating more things (*I can connect my accounting software to the bank and set up auto-responders*), and delegating others (*Someone else can write up this week's food order*). When determining what to delegate, it is helpful to determine what you really like doing and what you are really good at doing. If you are good at something and enjoy it, don't delegate that. It is part of what brings you joy in your work. If you aren't good at it and you dislike it, then find another way to get it done. Automate it or delegate it. As they say, *"Hire it done."* I challenge you to write a list of everything that you know you will be expected to do as a director. Write it all down. Then see what can be automated. Start there. Delegate to a computer. Sending out automated billing notices. If that is already set up, look into creating and automating a series of welcome emails for new families. Create it once and then have a computer carry it forward.

Create a grid like this and place all the items needing to be done within it. Things in which you are highly skilled but not particularly interested in doing go in the top left section. Those in which you are neither interested nor good at go below that. The top right quadrant is for the things that both give you pleasure, and you are good at. The bottom right corner is for things that you love to do, but you're not very good—For me, this is painting. Don't delegate things in the top right corner. That is your Zone of Genius. Delegate as much as you can out of the lower left corner.

Michael Hyatt's amazing book, *Free to Focus*, walks you through this editing and delegation process. It is a short, weekend read. If you are working 50 or more hours a week, you owe it to yourself to read it.

Remember The 7 P's

Prior planning prevents personal pathetically poor performance.

Delegating is something that will totally change your job and everyone else's, too. If done properly, it establishes an atmosphere where everyone wins. This means:

- More time for you
- Establishing an atmosphere of trust and respect
- Encouraging people to use their highest skills
- Promoting professionalism

Recap of How to Delegate:

1. Plan what needs to be delegated
2. Select the person
3. Meet with the person
4. Create a plan of action
5. Inform the other faculty members
6. Implement the plan
7. Follow up Remember to thank the person!

Branch Out

Brainstorm all of the duties you have or will have as director. Place those duties in the delegation grid. What will you be delegating today?

CHAPTER 7

Where Does the Time Go?

"Tiger Time. We call it that inside my business because I have to be fiercely protective of that time. You need to make sure the people in your house, or wherever you are, know that Tiger Time means you can't be interrupted, and you'll come out of the cave when the time is right."
–Amy Porterfield, author

There are days when you feel like you didn't get anything done. I have had many. Let me tell you about one of them. I was at a center where I had been hired to coach the director and improve her performance. She wasn't getting her business management tasks done, and it was affecting the performance of the school. I spent the first day observing so that I could devise a plan for improvement.

In all my days in childcare centers, I have never had a day like that one. It was a large center with a capacity of almost 200 children and an administrative team of three. There was a director, a curriculum coordinator, and an enrollment manager. An intercom system connected to all the classrooms so that teachers could buzz for help as needed. The administrators were never in the office. Okay, occasionally they were, but they were constantly being called out to deal with other people's monkeys. It was ridiculous. I used my tally sheet form to record the interruptions. There were 47 calls in 30 minutes. That is more than one every minute. No wonder the work wasn't getting done. Could your laser-focus be interrupted every minute? It was impossible. I'm just going to say it. *The director's time is more valuable than the classroom teachers.* This is not an opinion, and I am not being egocentric. This is a fact reflected by the paychecks. Directors are more valuable. As such, we have to protect our time. Of course, it has to be balanced with supporting the classrooms, but you have to have time to call parents, order supplies, pay bills, create and execute the business plan, hire and counsel staff, implement the marketing, and deal with the finances. None of the teachers can do those things. So, when you interrupt your work to take a teacher a Band-Aid, you are wasting valuable resources.

As a Girl Scout, I was taught to use resources wisely. Money and time count as valuable, limited resources. So is mental focus. All of these are squandered by endless calls from classrooms or visits from staff. Creating systems that encourage staff to take care of their own monkeys, get their own supplies, and facilitate better communication is the definite goal.

You need to be aware of how you manage your time, resources, and activities that you enjoy doing. Spreading yourself too thin, running out of time, and getting stuck on tasks that you dislike instead of doing what you enjoy can cause you to burn out.

Have you noticed yet how concerned I am with helping you NOT burn out? That is because this job is so freaking cool! It is one of the most rewarding jobs out there when it is done correctly. I want you to enjoy a long, pleasurable tenure as a director as I have.

The next steps of the journey are to start identifying some of the time-loss factors. Everyone uses timewasters every day. Examples are:

- Procrastination
- Idle time
- Daydreaming
- Inconsistency
- Absent mindedness
- A watch that is not accurate

- Doing other people's work Too much attention on small details
- Not having a schedule No self-imposed deadlines Lack of goals Relying on mental notes
- Too long on the telephone
- Reading junk mail
- Messy work areas No alone time to process
- Social media
- Pinterest

All of the time wasters listed are caused by lack of planning. The key to managing your time is planning your time. The less time that you feel you have, the more important it is to plan your time. Spending a few minutes planning at the beginning or end of each day will pay a reward of more time for you many times over.

The way to increase the amount of time available is to plan. Sometimes you feel so busy that it will appear that there isn't time to plan. This is exactly the reason to plan: to find more time. Some people choose to plan in the morning. This is good because you are fresh, energetic, less likely to get sidetracked, ready to tackle the day and ready to set goals.

Some people choose to plan in the evening. This is good because you have the day all set when you wake up. Your unconscious mind can work overnight on developing planned ideas, you know what you accomplished that day, you have a good perspective on deciding activities for tomorrow and it can alert time for you.

Working The Plan

Develop a daily schedule that your staff can count on. When will you visit with each of the classrooms? Walking through with a notebook or clipboard once in the morning and once in the afternoon works well. That way the staff sees your Monkey Containment Device (choose a special notebook), and they know that's the time that they can give you updates, ask questions, and make requests. You won't lose track of them all because now you have a place to put them.

You also want to have a weekly block schedule. I call this Tiger Time. I got the idea from Amy Porterfield. Tiger Time is time that you guard like a tiger would protect what is his. For instance, you might have an hour every Monday afternoon where you update files, or Thursday morning is set aside for financial matters. Put these large blocks into your schedule. Other things can go in around them. Your work building and maintaining the business of the school is IMPORTANT! Have a system to communicate to others that you are in Tiger Time. Tiger Time can be interrupted for true emergencies, not for a Band-Aid for little Josephina.

Once you have this basic framework, it is time to fill it in. This is where the to-do list comes into play. Leave room for the things that come up each day like parent conversations, phone calls, and other duties. Start off with four or five items on your daily to-do list.

Each Day

1. List and review goals for the week
2. Write a to-do list
3. Break down complex tasks into smaller, easier tasks
4. Prioritize Identify tasks that can be delegated
5. Update as the day progresses

There is a tool called the Unscheduled Schedule. It is designed to look at your use of time. Write down what you think your schedule will look like. Then for a week, write down what happened over the week. Every 15 minutes just jot down what you did since the last entry. When the time is up, compare the results. It will be quite illuminating.

Planning and scheduling will work for you. It is best to try a variety of methods to find one that best suits you and your personality.

If four or five items per day seem ridiculous, please remember that is not everything you will do—just what you planned to do. You will also have a running list of things that need to be done.

The running to-do list can get long. By prioritizing each item, you can get the things that need to get done first and can productively check things off the list.

Assign priorities to each task. First, you will need to do some triage; doing this on the fifteenth of the month works well. Triage is a three-step process of sorting:

1. Tasks that will be completed only with my intervention (my monkey)
2. Tasks that will be completed without my intervention (not my monkey)
3. Tasks that will not be successful regardless of my intervention (remove from my list)

Once you have triaged your list, it is time to set the priorities:

- Top Priority – those tasks that need to be done as soon as possible
- High Priority – those tasks to be done within two days
- Medium Priority – those tasks that need to be done this week
- Low Priority – those tasks that need to be completed in a week or more

Look at your list of priorities. Which lights you up and brings joy to your life? If that thing or things are low on your list, then perhaps the reason you're not productive is the conflict between what your heart wants and what your mind wants. Spend some time sorting out this piece, and you'll find that perhaps you can care less about your work identity. This will likely free up time and space to serve your parenting priority or your "inner whittler."

Once you have your priorities in alignment, see which you need to attend to now, which can wait, and which can be dropped. Still tying your sixteen-year-old's sneakers? Trust me… You can let that go. Obsessively worrying about next Christmas? Yeah, that can wait. Fixing the hole in the roof? Now that's a Now Thing.

There is no point in being busy for the sake of being busy. It's all wasted movement that generates nothing as stated so eloquently in The Tragedy of Macbeth, Act 5, Scene 5, by William Shakespeare:

> *...Life's but a walking shadow, a poor player*
> *That struts and frets his hour upon the stage*
> *And then is heard no more: it is a tale*
> *Told by an idiot, full of sound and fury,*

Signify something. Drop the busyness in favor of efficient productivity.

Branch Out

Block out your schedule. What are the tasks you need to do without interruption? When will you do them?

CHAPTER 8

Who Is My Best Self?

"Everyone is a genius. But if you judge a fish by its ability to climb a tree, it will live its whole life believing that it is stupid."–Albert Einstein

I want you to absolutely ROCK this position. I want you to be an amazing director. You can be if you are true to your best self. What do I mean by being true to yourself? Acknowledge who you are and what makes you tick. This goes into lots of different areas. The more you get to know yourself and what your strengths and weaknesses are, the better director and the better overall human being you will be. I have been directing for many, many years, but one year will always stand out for me.

One year during the Week of the Young Child, the parents not only organized to give recognition to the teachers, but they also did one for me. They put together a thank-you card on foam core that had pictures of the kids having a great time at the center over the previous year. They thanked me for all the work I did to make the center what it was. They thanked me for making it the community that they were happy to bring their children to everyday. This was the one and only time that parents recognized me. It has been more than a decade since then, and I still have that poster. It is hanging in my office right now.

This simple gesture resonated with me so much because of my love language. The way that I feel appreciated and valued is through deeds of service. I let the people in my program know that I care about them by doing things for them. That day I finally felt appreciated by the parents because they created something with their own hands. They took their time to create a thing for me. They did a deed of service. The more we know about how we feel appreciated, how we learn, how we lead, and how we hold tension, the better we can run our programs. It's okay to let your staff know how you like to receive recognition. Ask them how they like to receive recognition. Find out as much as you can about them while still maintaining professional distance.

Love Languages

Gary Chapman popularized the concept of love languages in his book The 5 Love Languages: The Secret to Love the Lasts. He further expanded the concept to address other relationships. The key element is that people have different types of motivation, which he called love languages. According to Chapman, the desire to be loved is our deepest human desire, and one that is often left unmet due to the differences in the way we express and receive love. He explains that in order for us to feel as though our deep-seated need for love is met, the love that we receive must make sense to us. Whether it's a pat on the back, an award for a job well done, or some one-on-one time, we each have unique emotions attached to what makes us feel appreciated.

Motivation is maximized when people receive their ideal form of praise, encouragement, or reward for their efforts. Since it is the job of a director to not only keep the center running but also to keep up a happy workforce, understanding what makes individuals tick is crucial for helping the bottom line.

The Five Languages of Appreciation are:

1. Words of Affirmation – uses words to affirm people
2. Acts of Service – actions speak louder than words
3. Receiving Gifts – people like things to feel appreciated

4. Quality Time – giving someone undivided attention
5. Physical Touch – appropriate touch (pats on the back)

By determining which one applies to you, you can set yourself up for success. There are many self-assessments available to determine which language best fits. Sharing this information with those who work closest with you, those who report directly to you or to whom you report. It will aid your team in offering you the support you need.

If a director can properly create and maintain a happy workplace, team members will seamlessly work together, be more productive, and more engaged. By showing your appreciation in a way that resonates with an individual staff member, you improve the job satisfaction and the culture at your center.

Part of this is determining the love language of your staff. Having a staff training about the love languages and how to use them in your classrooms allows the staff to see the impact of this concept. Your teachers also want to encourage each other. The knowledge of each other's languages will improve the efficacy of that encouragement.

Learning Styles

As an adult learner, it is good to know what kind of learner you are as well as how to teach to all learning styles. This is important when you are doing staff training, sharing information with your parents, and even more importantly, for your staff to understand about their students.

There is an old saying:

I hear and I forget, I see and I remember.
I do and I learn, I teach and I know.
I read and I understand.

Different people have different learning preferences that stem from how they learn best. There is no right or wrong way to learn. The three basic learning styles are:

- Visual – learning by looking at images
- Auditory – learning by listening
- Kinesthetic – learning by experiencing and doing

Most children start out as kinesthetic learners and then develop visual strengths around the third grade and auditory skills around fifth grade. Interestingly, Western cultures tend to have more visual learners and fewer auditory ones.

Although everyone uses all three of these modes of learning at some level, people tend to rely on one mode more than another. To determine your particular learning style, read the "Modes of Learning-Which Do You Prefer?" chart on the pages to follow. Check the boxes that best describe the way you prefer to learn, remember, solve problems, communicate, use language, and so on. The category with the most checks is your primary learning style.

The Basic Learning Process

This training system follows a structure that accommodates all individual learning styles. This structure called is a five-step progression of activities designed to meet the learner's needs, interaction, relevance, self-direction and practicality, while accommodating all three learning styles.

The five steps of the Basic Learning Process are as follows:

1. Understand why the skill is important.
2. Discuss the specific behaviors involved in the skill.
3. Watch a demonstration of the skill.
4. Practice the skill.
5. Use the skill.

Modes of Learning-Which Do You Prefer?

Visual Learners

- **Learning:** Learns by seeing; benefits from demonstrations. Forms mental picture to make sense of what is happening.
- **Memory:** Remembers faces, forgets names. Takes notes and looks at them. Recalls colors and shapes easily.
- **Problem Solving:** Is deliberate; plans in advance. Organizes thoughts by writing them. Keeps lists of problems or things to do.
- **Communication:** Can talk quickly, but rarely at length. Becomes impatient if extensive listening is required.
- **Language:** Uses visual words such as see, look and watch. "I see what you mean." "I see it clearly now."
- **Other:** Is affected by color of room and order or chaos. Seldom gets lost.

Auditory Learners

- **Learning:** Learns by seeing; benefits from demonstrations. Forms mental picture to make sense of what is happening.
- **Memory:** Remembers names, forgets faces. Remembers by hearing the repeating.
- **Problem Solving:** Talks problems out or thinks them through verbally. Talks to self. Can go around and around before deciding.
- **Communication:** Enjoys listening, but sometimes cannot wait to talk. Goes into long, detailed descriptions. Uses internal dialogue to work through problems.
- **Language:** Uses verbal words such as ask, listen, hear, tell... "That rings a bell." "I hear you."
- **Other:** Speaks with a melodious voice. Does not always trust feelings. Likes music.

Kinesthetic Learners

- **Learning:** Learns by doing and hands-on interest. Feels way through experiences. Understands big picture before detail.
- **Memory:** Remembers events, forgets details. Takes notes, but does not look at them.
- **Problem Solving:** Attacks problems physically. Impulsive; often selects solutions involving greatest activity. Needs guidance through steps of a problem.
- **Communication:** Gestures when speaking. Does not listen well; stands close while speaking or listening, paces to think. Frequently pauses while speaking. Is unclear about body language.
- **Language:** Uses action words such as get, take, make and understand. "I get the picture." "I feel good about that."
- **Other:** Can't sit still long. Should sit where it won't bother others. Listens better if touched.

Management Styles

Everyone has a style. The way you walk, dress, talk and move are your style. There are dozens of theories on personality, management, leadership and communication styles. As a childcare professional you need to understand how your different roles will also have different styles. As the director of a program, you will have a style that works best with parents, a style that works best with staff, and most likely a style that works best with children in your program.

We are going to look at different management and leadership styles as they relate to working with your staff. First, we are going to look at four personality styles that are described in the language of management. The Producer This is the individual who has the drive and the discipline necessary to see real results produced. Impatient, active, and always busy, the Producer has little time for idle chit-chat. Direct and to the point, typical Producers are behind-the scenes movers and shakers. Many Producers are attracted to high-intensity sales departments. They are too busy to "waste time" with meetings. They prefer to cut the small talk and get out there to get the job done.

The Administrator

This personality ensures that rules are in place and followed, that plans are made and adhered to. Precise and accurate, the Administrator creates methods and procedures to make sure things are done "right." Analytical and logical, Administrators clean up other people's carelessness. They like to keep the organization humming at a steady pace and are willing to do things more slowly and carefully. Administrators are drawn to tasks that require systemic thinking and precision, such as accounting.

The Entrepreneur

This personality is an ideas person, always asking "why?" or "why not?" A visionary with dreams, plans and schemes, the Entrepreneur leads others to ideas that they would not pursue on their own. Success for an Entrepreneur requires both creativity and risk. They sometimes get bored with short-term tasks and prefer developing the long-term vision. Entrepreneurs are often charismatic, and generate ideas for new projects, new approaches to problems, or even new businesses.

The Integrator

This personality is people oriented. True Integrators value social harmony and thrive on peacemaking and teamwork. The Integrator's pleasantness is unmistakable. Amiable and empathetic, the Integrator is the first to cooperate in helping with tasks or problems. They prefer to work by consensus instead of taking a strong position against others. Integrators are attracted to people-oriented occupations like human resources.

Tension

Where we hold our tension can vary greatly. The four primary places where people hold their tension are:

- Jaw

- Neck/Shoulder
- Hands
- Hips & Gluteus maximus (that's right—even there)

Let's look at these individually.

People who hold their tension in their jaw and neck are more likely to chew gum or bite their nails as a form of tension release. As children they were more likely to be habitual biters or angry biters. In elementary school their pencils probably looked like termites got to them. Tension headaches and, to some extent, migraines are tied to people who hold tension in their jaw and neck. If you use a night guard because you grind your teeth at night, there is a good chance that this is where you hold your tension

Holding tension in your shoulders is a little bit different. Holding tension in your shoulders has a tendency to make you appear rigid. You don't move your arms completely when you are having a conversation. People who hold their tension in their shoulders have a tendency to shrug or hunch their shoulders forward when they are stressed. Holding tension in your shoulders has a tendency to lead to back pain. As children, holding tension in your shoulders often results in knocking into things and/or wanting to punch or hit things. The incredible release of tension when you're able to strike something with your whole arm helps to release the tension in your shoulders. A great stress reliever for people who hold their tension in their shoulders is taking up something like a boxing class or Zumba.

We all know someone who holds their tension in their hands. They are the people who at a stressful meeting should never be given a retractable ballpoint pen. They click it again and again and again without even seeming to notice that they do. Drawing, doodling, and working with dough are all activities that a person who holds tension in their hands may do when under pressure. They're also more likely to clasp their hands together when in a difficult situation. Or perhaps fold their hands into V. As a child a person who holds tension in their hands might spend an enormous amount of time at the sink washing hands, playing in the water, and any kind of texture play. These types of activities where they can really move their hands and release the tension in their hands. Play-Doh is an amazing tension reliever for children who hold their tension in their hands. Those hand-gripping exercisers are the most acceptable adult substitutes. The last place that people hold tension is in their lower body, their hips or their rear end. Stomping is a key indicator of someone who holds tension in their lower body. If kicking a soccer ball was one of the greatest joys of your life because of how relaxed you felt at the end of a game, then you probably hold your attention in your lower body. That person who when you're out to dinner is constantly jostling their leg and therefore jostling the whole table, that person holds their tension in their lower body. As a child this manifests as kicking, stomping, and pushing things with their legs.

The reason you need to figure this out is because you need to know what to do to relieve the tension before it gets to the boiling point—whether it's you, a staff member, or a child under stress. So, if you know that you hold tension in your lower body, then go for a walk or a run. If you know that you hold tension in your hands, go make bread. Use scissors to cut out file folder games. If you know that you hold tension in your jaw, then sing. Eat some beef jerky. If you hold the tension in your shoulders, then join a softball team. Do some yoga stretches.

The more you know about how your staff holds tension, the easier it is to work with them when you have a conflict or when you need to counsel them. If they hold their tension in their hands, have them take notes on a piece of paper. it will help to relieve some of their tension. If they hold their tension in their lower body walk with them around the playground while you're counseling them.

You're going to have rough day as the director. You need to be able to relieve that tension so that you can do your job.

Branch Out

Answer the following in writing:
What is my love language?
What is my primary learning style?
What is my management style?
Where do I hold tension?

Awaken the Leader in You

Ten easy steps to developing your leadership skills by Sharif Khan The miracle power that elevates the few is to be found in their industry, application and perseverance, under the promptings of a brave determined spirit... Mark Twain Many motivational experts like to say that leaders are made, not born. I would argue the exact opposite. I believe we are all natural born leaders but have been deprogrammed along the way. As children we were natural leaders; curious, humble, always hungry and thirsty for knowledge, with an incredibly vivid imagination. We knew exactly what we wanted, were persistent and determined in getting what we wanted, and had the ability to motivate, inspire and influence everyone around us to help us in accomplishing our mission. So why is this so difficult to do as adults? What happened? As children–over time–we got used to hearing, "No," "Don't," "Can't," "No!" "Don't do this," "Don't do that," "You can't do this," "You can't do that," "No!" Many of our parents told us to keep quiet and not disturb the adults by asking silly questions. This pattern continued into high school with our teachers telling us what we could and couldn't do and what was possible. Then many of us got hit with the big one: institutionalized formal education known as college or university. Unfortunately, the traditional educational system doesn't teach students how to become leaders; it teaches students how to become polite order takers for the corporate world. Instead of learning to become; creative, independent, self-reliant, and to think for themselves, most people learn how to obey and intelligently follow rules to keep the corporate machine humming. Developing the Leader in you to live your highest life then requires a process of unlearning by self-remembering and self-honoring. Being an effective leader again will require you to be brave and unlock the door to your inner attic, where your childhood dreams lie, going inside to the heart. Based on my research in the area of human development and leadership, here are ten easy steps you can take to awaken the leader in you and rekindle your passion for greatness: 1. Humility. Leadership starts with humility. To be a highly successful leader, you must first humble yourself like a little child and be willing to serve others. Nobody wants to follow someone who is arrogant. Be humble as a child, always curious, always hungry and thirsty for knowledge. For what is excellence but knowledge plus knowledge plus knowledge–always wanting to better yourself, always improving, always growing. When you are humble, you become genuinely interested in people because you want to learn from them. And because you want to learn and grow, you will be a far more effective listener, which is the #1 leadership communication tool. When people sense you are genuinely interested in them, and in listening to them, they will naturally be interested in you and listen to what you have to say. 2. S.W.O.T. is an acronym for Strengths, Weaknesses, Opportunities, and Threats. Although it's a strategic management tool taught at Stanford and Harvard Business Schools–and used by large multinationals–it can just as effectively be used in your own professional development as a leader. This is a useful key to gain access to self-knowledge, self-remembering, and self-honoring.

Start by listing all your Strengths including your accomplishments. Then write down all your Weaknesses and what needs to be improved. Make sure to include any doubts, anxieties, fears and worries that you may have. These are the demons and dragons guarding the door to your inner attic. By bringing them to conscious awareness you can begin to slay them. Then proceed by listing all the Opportunities you see available to you for using your strengths. Finally, write down all the Threats or obstacles that are currently blocking you, or that you think you will encounter along the way to achieving your dreams. 3. Follow Your Bliss. Regardless of how busy you are, always take time to do what you love doing. Being an alive and vital person vitalizes others. When you are pursuing your passions, people around you cannot help but feel impassioned by your presence. This will make you a charismatic leader. Whatever it is that you enjoy doing; be it writing, acting, painting, drawing, photography, sports, reading, dancing, networking, or working on entrepreneurial ventures. Set aside time every week, ideally two or three hours a day, to pursue these activities. Believe me, you'll find the time. If you were to video tape yourself for a day, you would be shocked to see how much time goes to waste! 4. Dream Big. If you want to be larger than life, you need a dream that's larger than life. Small dreams won't serve you or anyone else. It takes the same amount of time to dream small than it does to dream big. So be Big and be Bold! Write down your One Biggest Dream, the one that excites you the most. Remember; don't be small and realistic, be bold and unrealistic! Go for the Gold, the Pulitzer, the Nobel, the Oscar and the highest you can possibly achieve in your field. After you've written down your dream, list every single reason why you CAN achieve your dream instead of worrying about why you can't. 5. Vision. Without a vision, we perish. If you can't see yourself winning that award and feel the tears of triumph streaming down your face, it's unlikely you will be able to lead yourself or others to victory. Visualize what it would be like accomplishing your dream. See it, smell it, taste it, hear it and feel it in your gut. 6. Perseverance. Victory belongs to those who want it the most and stay in it the longest. Now that you have a dream, make sure you take consistent action every day. I recommend doing at least 5 things every day that will move you closer to your dream. 7. Honor Your Word. Every time you break your word, you lose power. Successful leaders keep their word and their promises. You can accumulate all the toys and riches in the world, but you only have one reputation in life. Your word is gold. Honor it. 8. Get a Mentor. Find yourself a mentor, preferably someone who has already achieved a high degree of success in your field. Don't be afraid to ask. You've got nothing to lose. www.mentoring.com is an excellent mentoring website and a great resource for finding local mentoring programs. They even have a free personal profile you can fill out in order to potentially find you a suitable mentor. In addition to mentors, take time to study autobiographies of great leaders that you admire. Learn everything you can from their lives and model some of their successful behaviors. 9. Be Yourself. Use your relationships with mentors and your research on great leaders as models or reference points to work from, but never copy or imitate them like a parrot. Everyone has vastly different leadership styles. History books are filled with leaders who are; soft-spoken, introverted and quiet, all the way to the other extreme of being outspoken, extroverted, loud and everything in between. A quiet and simple Gandhi or a soft-spoken peanut farmer named Jimmy Carter (who became president of the United States and won a Nobel Peace Prize) have been just as effective world leaders as a loud and flamboyant Winston Churchill, or the tough leadership style employed by, "The Iron Lady," Margaret Thatcher. I admire Hemingway as a writer. But if I copy Hemingway, I'd be a second- or third-rate Hemingway at best, instead of a first-rate Sharif. Be yourself, your best self. Always competing against yourself and bettering yourself, you will become a first rate YOU instead of a second rate somebody else. 10. Give. Finally, be a giver. Leaders are givers. By giving, you activate a universal law as sound as gravity: Life gives to the giver and takes from the taker. The more you give, the more you get. If you want more love, respect, support and compassion, give love, respect, support and compassion. Be a mentor to others. Give back to your community. As a leader, the only way to get what you want is by helping enough people get what they want first. As Sir Winston Churchill once said, "We make a living by what we get; we make a life by what we give." Sharif Khan is a professional speaker and author of the highly acclaimed, Psychology of the Hero Soul, an inspirational book on awakening the Hero within and developing peoples leadership potential. You can reach him at sharif@herosoul.com or visit www.HeroSoul.com

SECTION II

CHAPTER 9

Which Parents Belong at Your Center?

"Coming together is the beginning. Keeping together is progress. Working together is success."- Henry Ford

• Now repeat after me. Your future self will thank you for it: *I want parents who match my center. I need parents who look at things the same way I do. I cannot make every parent happy.*

With that being said, how do we present ourselves? How our program smells, sounds, and looks will attract some parents and repel others. That is good! Imagine you are a prospective parent, and you go into tour two very different programs:

Program A

Program A is loud. It uses an eclectic model. It takes some methods from traditional schools and some from Reggio Emilia. That means that the children are actively exploring and interacting with their environment. For some parents, this is unacceptable: a sign of low quality. They want to see children working quietly at tables. Are those parents your parents? If this is not the type of program you offer, make sure you let the parents know. Educate them about how you measure quality and where you get your information.

Program B

Program B uses the Montessori Method, which stresses a quiet and contemplative classroom. This is also a quality classroom with children exploring their abilities. The materials are set out around the room, and children work alone or in pairs primarily. If a parent is looking for active social involvement and many interactions, they may not see this in Program B. That does not mean it is not exceptional. This program will need to educate parents on the virtues of Montessori programs.

In both of these situations, the class size, space available, materials available, the ratio of children to caregivers, and the caregivers' knowledge will be evaluated. In addition to these, there needs to be good communication between parents and staff. Does the parent feel comfortable talking to you and the teachers? There has to be a genuine relationship between the caregivers and the families.

One way to find good matches for your program is by observing and expanding how people find you. If many people see your center when they drive by, then the outside of your center needs to tell the story of what type of program you have. If most clients find you from referrals, then be sure to give your current clients enough information to share with people who share their values. All of your documentation, print materials, website, and social media presence need to reflect your values and educational philosophy. If people are finding your center primarily through web searches, then position yourself to attract the clients that are a good match—like iron to a lodestone. It would also help if you could repel those who are not a good fit. Some parents will prefer the busy, play-based program, and others will select the focused, self-directed learning type of program. So how do you define your ideal parents? Or as the marketing world calls them, your parallel clients—your ideal customer avatar?

 When parallel parent finds a program, it is because they see or hear something that resonates with them. They have either witnessed media where you present the type of school you are or they heard about you from someone they know, like, and trust. A referral could come from parents who have been to your center, whether they enrolled or not, and tell their friends about your program. Many times, people came to my program because someone they knew who toured was not a good match but told friends about my program because it would be a good match for them. Having a good referral program is one of the smartest marketing decisions you can ever make. We will be talking about marketing more in a later section.

 When you're dealing with your ideal customer or your parallel parent, you'll notice that orientation and tours go very differently than when you're dealing with a client who is not a good match for you—a perpendicular parent. The latter asks you questions that you don't have satisfying answers to. The things that concern them are not the most problematic things for you and your staff. For instance, if a parent is very concerned about their child developing social graces by saying, "yes, ma'am" and "no, sir," then they're going to ask questions about how you are teaching manners and respect. If you don't have a good answer for that because that is not a focus for your program, then this is a sign that this parent is not a good match.

On the other hand, if this is part of your focus because you feel that social graces are an essential part of preparing children for school, then you will have good answers for how you are teaching that. Again, I am not suggesting that you please all parents and have good answers to every question. I am saying that a parallel parent will ask the questions that you have also thought about and are concerned with; therefore, you will have good answers. The parent that is not a match, however, will ask questions that seem like they come out of left field.

Orientations

Getting to Know Each Other Once a family comes through the tour and enrolls, now it is time for orientation. What does orientation look like at your program? How is the family going to get oriented? How will they know where to hang up their child's bag or tote? Where will they get information from you? Is there an app that they need to sign up for? All of these are questions that need to be addressed in some form of the orientation process. It can all be done in a variety of ways: in person at a welcome-to-school night, over a week via email and video tours, or a combination of both. There is no one right answer that fits every program. However, there is one right way for you to do orientation at your school right now. You need to think through what that process should be. The orientation process will help to confirm with the right-fit client that you are the right-fit program for them. They are not left out in the dark about setting up an observation day, bringing the child another change of clothes without causing disruption, or a hundred other questions that may be running through their minds. Whatever questions they have, they would be addressed during the orientation process. In reality, the orientation or onboarding process for the parents takes between six weeks and three months. It takes that long for them to feel secure at your center, to feel connected and bonded with you and your teachers. Your orientation process should take the time frame into account. You also want to take any opportunity to surprise and delight them throughout the onboarding period to ensure that they are well bonded to your program. Sending a welcome package to their home with a center handbook and a backpack (or whatever works for your budget) can be a significant part of the orientation process. Parallel parents will also make friends with the other parents at your center, creating a cohesive community that you can then leverage through an active Parent Teacher Association or Organization. Parents who have similar values can support one another in this critical work to raise the next generation. They are more likely to want to have play dates together on weekends or holidays. The more you can bring in the right-fit client, the more support each child will have because not only will they have you and the teachers and their parents, but they'll also have the parents of the other children in the class all supporting them in there to become the best them they can be.

Parents who have similar values will participate more in your program than wrong-fit clients. They will want to come to your parent workshops; they'll bring their child to your parents' night out programs. They will come to your workdays; they will fill out surveys. They will be more invested. They will participate in the winter holiday festival or special events for Mother's Day or Father's Day. They will invite their friends to come to your Spring Fling Dance. We look for this when we try to match our programs with parents whose views are parallel to our centers' cultures.

It is also essential to talk about these wrong-fit clients. When these parents enroll in your program because it's the right location or the correct price or their friend told them to come, they didn't choose it because it matches what they want for their child. Those parents will be much more of an emotional drain on your program. They're going to be the ones that nitpick the updates from your teachers, who second-guess your policies, who misbehave and encourage others to do the same. They are fundamentally unhappy with your program, even if they don't know it, because your school does not match their core values. It does not mean that they are a terrible family. It does not mean that you have a lousy program. It just means that the two do not match up. There is an excellent exercise for exploring your parallel and perpendicular parents in the free workbook that you can download. (texasdirector.org/workbook) You're going to describe your ideal customer and take a little bit of a mental journey about what your program would be like if you had more of those perfect clients and fewer of the wrong-fit clients.

Happy Clients Generate Referrals and Repeats

1. 1. If you make a promise, keep it—regardless of cost!
2. 2. If you cannot make good on your promise, let the client know as soon as possible.
3. 3. Answer phones promptly—no more than three rings.
4. 4. Don't make people wait.

5. 5. Communicate. Assume the client knows nothing.
6. 6. Encourage honest feedback.
7. 7. Sell only what the client needs.

Branch Out

Describe a family you have worked with that would be a wrong-fit client.

PARENT RESOURCE

Child Care: What to Look For

When you place your child in the care of someone else, be it family childcare, a center, a relative, or a friend, the key to your peace of mind is trust. The more you trust the caregiver, the more secure you will feel. Here are some questions to ask: Does the center:

- Have child-rearing attitudes similar to yours?
- Have the training to understand what children can and want to do at different stages of growth?
- Spend time holding, playing with, and talking to the children?
- Have enough time to look after all the children in its care?
- Welcome visits from parents at any time?

Does the center have:

- A license?
- Only a few children? Remember, children do better in small groups.
- A clean and comfortable look?
- Equipment that is safe and in good repair?
- Nutritious meals and snacks?

- Are there chances for the children to:
- Be held, cuddled, smiled at, and talked to?
- Relax and rest when they need to?
- Explore safely?
- Play with objects that develop their senses of touch, sight, and hearing?
- Learn language through the caregiver's talking to the child: naming things, describing what he or she is doing, and responding to the child's actions?

CHAPTER 10

What About Ages & Stages?

"If you never jumped from one sofa to another to avoid lava, you've never had a childhood."- Anonymous

Child development rarely proceeds as one might expect. In countless books, we read that it steadily progresses from one thing to another in a neatly set, scheduled order. Oh, if only it were that predictable. I worked in an infant room with eight babies that I knew pretty well, ranging from about two months to 12-months-old. The lead teacher and the assistant were talking about who would be moving up to the toddler room. Part of the discussion involved one of the children would probably not be moving up with his two best friends because he was not walking yet. Now let me tell you a little bit about this boy, Rodrigo. He was as smart as a whip. His parents were bilingual and wanted to raise him as bilingual; they primarily spoke to him in Portuguese. He had a much more extensive receptive and expressive vocabulary in English than was typical for an 11-month-old child. Also, he had a receptive and expressive vocabulary of about the same size in Portuguese. He was doing what his parents wanted, learning two languages simultaneously, and learning them well. He was speaking in complete sentences, short but complete.

Rodrigo was in the room while these teachers discussed how the two other infants, he played with would be changing classrooms most of the time. He was rolling and crawling but not showing any signs of walking. They, of course, thought nothing of it. You don't think anything of infants overhearing your conversations. I probably wouldn't have thought anything of it either if it weren't for what happened in the next three days. Rodrigo stopped talking. He also did something else, something remarkable. He stopped crawling, started pulling up and walking along every surface he could find. Mind you, this is the same child who weeks before repeatedly let go of the teacher's hands when they pulled him up to a standing position. He'd much rather drop to his knees and crawl.

Rodrigo knew how to crawl, and he did it well. In fact, he could travel faster by crawling than his playmates could by walking unsteadily on their two feet. However, upon hearing that his friends would move up without him—which, by the way, a child of that age should not have been able to understand—Rodrigo decided that he needed to walk. So, he turned off the part of the brain that was working so hard to understand and process two languages and instead applied that brainpower to learning how to walk. I have no other explanation for what happened in those three days. He did not say a single word, not to us and not to his parents. But within two weeks, Rodrigo was walking and happy and moving up with his two best friends into the toddler classroom.

Rodrigo's case illustrates that development does not take a smooth course. Children don't progress as predicted in any of the charts you will see in this book and other books. They develop in fits and starts based on their interests and the opportunities given to them. One area's progression may lead to regression or falling back in another area. Rodrigo could not continue acquiring language while acquiring the motor skills needed to walk. There's only so much mental energy that he had, and he had to apply it to the most important thing at that time. This is why I frequently saw children suck their thumb again after not doing it at all for six months when they're going through toilet training. They have so much mental energy, and they cannot use the energy for self-soothing when they're also using it to monitor and control their bodies' functions.

Child development functions much like ripples of raindrops in a pond. The ripples interact with each other. Some ripples get bigger faster, and we can't control how quickly each ripple grows. We can only provide the pond and watch this water dance unfold.

Preparing the Pond

Let's take a little bit of time to explore some child development basics to help create the best environment for those ripples to roll smoothly.

Hundreds of books have been written about these, so we are not going to write a complete text on ages and stages. Rather, this section is designed to give a snapshot and put your ideas into the normative development for different age ranges. If you are new to the field or feel that you do not have enough information on a specific age group, please attend training or read books regarding the age group about which you think you need more understanding. You can also visit the internet, local library, watch good training videos or just spend time observing the children in your program. It is essential to recognize what is expected and what is above and below the normal curve. Four basic principles cover development throughout childhood. Development generally progresses from:

- The top of the body down the trunk
- The body's core to the extremities
- Large motor skills to fine motor skills
- Concrete concepts to abstract concepts

Examples of Top to Bottom Development

- The child's development starts at the top of the body and progresses down the trunk to the end of the feet. Along with center to extremities and large to fine motor development, this process explains motor development progression. While deviations do occur, this is the description of typical development: Neck control before shoulder control
- Purposeful eye movement before intentional mouth movement

- Rolling over, in which the child can turn shoulders first and then hips
- Can control eating before eliminating

Examples of Center to Extremities Development

- Can swing arm before flipping hand
- Crawling (hip joint movement) before walking (ankle movement)
  Smell is the first sense to fully develop; the last is touch
- Accuracy with hammering (shoulder movement) before accuracy
  with a paintbrush (finger movement)

Examples of Large Motor to Fine Motor Skills

- Swallowing liquids to chewing and swallowing solids
- Finger painting to calligraphy
- Kicking a soccer ball to playing hacky sack
- Crawling (thighs and other large muscle movement) to walking
  (foot placement and balance throughout the body)

Examples of Concrete to Abstract Concepts

- Infants need dolls to hold; school-aged children can have virtual pets
- Development of object permanence: things that are seen and touched
  are real- things and can exist outside of my area of perception; things
  can also exist that I have no sensory information about
- One-to-one correspondence before algebra
- Some rocks are crystals is understood before the rock cycle can
  be grasped

Children progress through various stages of development in a predictable
pattern. They generally follow the same steps and arrive at the same place:
functional adulthood. However, there will be variations in the timing of
the steps. While some children progress steadily from stage to stage, others
move forward in fits and starts. Some children go steadily in all areas as

others seem to put other areas on hold while moving forward in a particular area. Fortunately, all of this is normal.

The areas of development are:

- Fine Motor
- Gross Motor
- Cognitive
- Verbal
- Self-Help
- Social/Emotional
- Self-Concept/Spiritual

We will be focusing on the first six of these areas. There are many ways to break down children's development from birth to 12 years. We will use one-year age brackets for the first five years and then go in two/three-year groups for the remainder for ease of use.

It is essential to know what the children are developmentally ready for and how to support their growth. The developmental stages are predictable and sequential. The specific age that a child reaches any specific milestone depends on their ability and support of their environment. Knowing these norms of development will also help you spot variations. Here are sketches of the developmental milestones for different ages:

Infant Development1 year old

Fine Motor	Self Help
• Build 3 block tower • Clap hands	• Feed self with spoon • Drink from a cup
Gross Motor • Walking Sit to play with toys	**Social/Emotional** • Begins to understand ownership • Parallel play
Cognitive • Dump & fill (object permanence) • Attention span begins to expand	**Self Concept/ Spiritual** • Has friends • Growing independence "my do it"
Verbal • Power words "mine" "no" • Asks to get needs met "more"	**Specific Challenges** • Separation anxiety • Biting

2 years old

Fine Motor	Self Help
• First stage of drawing • Transfer games to develop grasp	• Helps with diapering/toileting • Undresses
Gross Motor • Runs • Sit and talk riding toys	**Social/Emotional** • Understands ownership • Starts labeling emotions
Cognitive • Sorting Cause & effect tester	**Self Concept/ Spiritual** • Dramatic play of family • Strong need for approval
Verbal • Increased use of verbs • Use of time words "lasterday"	**Specific Challenges** • Biting • Toilet learning

3 years old

Fine Motor	Self Help
• Can stand briefly on 1 foot • Feeds self well with utensils	• Toilet trained • Can dress self (except buttons)
Gross Motor	**Social/Emotional**
• Tricycles Climb stairs/ladder alternating feet	• Management of emotions improves • Dramatic play includes wider world
Cognitive	**Self Concept/ Spiritual**
• Fascinated with opposites • Learning to count	• Talents/interests become identity • Notice when others are different
Verbal	**Specific Challenges**
• 5-7 word sentence the norm • Asks friends to join play	• Toilet learning • Excluding classmates

4 years old

Fine Motor	Self Help
• Use scissors well • Starting to write words	• Can do buttons • Brushes teeth
Gross Motor	**Social/Emotional**
• Skipping • Pumping on swing	• Concerned with fairness • Interested in gender roles
Cognitive	**Self Concept/ Spiritual**
• Developing story telling skills • Understands gradiation	• Self concept tied to peer group • Works to perfect a drawing/activity
Verbal	**Specific Challenges**
• Enjoys rhyming • Retelling story books w/own words	• Tattling • Story telling

5years old

Fine Motor	Self Help
• Completes complex puzzles • Can write smoothly	• Ties shoe laces • Uses knife
Gross Motor	**Social/Emotional**
• Dances to music • Wants to take physical risks	• Knows home address/ phone • Shares with others
Cognitive	**Self Concept/ Spiritual**
• Builds complex structures • Understand the use of prepositions	• Meets visitors without shyness • Can articulate needs to friends
Verbal	**Specific Challenges**
• Speaks fluently • Knows age and birthday	• Cliques • School readiness

Lower elementary 6-8

Fine Motor	Self Help
• Copying designs and shapes • Skilled at scissors & small tools	• Ritual established (morning, bed) • Punishment avoidance
Gross Motor	**Social/Emotional**
• Good sense of balance • Can catch small balls	• Has a rigid view of right/wrong • Seeks security in groups
Cognitive	**Self Concept/ Spiritual**
• The lawyer is born - negotiates • Enjoys planning elaborate games	• Developing humor • Takes on responsibilities
Verbal	**Specific Challenges**
• Like to talk • Uses language often to retell stories	• Teasing • Rough play

Upper Elementary 9-12

Fine Motor	Self Help
• Can play ball games well • Handwriting improves (set by 15)	• Often careless of clothes • Developing tidiness standard
Gross Motor	**Social/Emotional**
• Bicycle riding proficiently • Endurance increases	• Strong interests & hobbies • Empathizes more with others
Cognitive	**Self Concept/ Spiritual**
• Questions real "are aliens are real?" • Ask thoughtful question	• Strong need to differentiate • Exploring the reasons for bad things
Verbal	**Specific Challenges**
• Starts to play with curse words • Greater use of the subjunctive case	• Girls have large growth spurt • Pre-pubescence

Within the first three years, the need to detect deficiencies is critical. Many of the "sensitive periods" of children's overall development happen during this period. Sensitive periods are periods when people can most easily acquire a skill or progress to the next developmental level. For instance, it is easiest to learn a language before entering puberty. Adults can learn new languages, but it much more difficult. Uneven or delayed development can result in life-long learning challenges without services. If delays are noted and the child receives services, it is often possible to recover most or even all of the delay. If the deficiency cannot be alleviated, however, then the coping mechanisms can become so ingrained as to make them second nature.

If you suspect a delay or aberrant ability, document your findings and discuss your concerns with the parents. Hopefully, the parents will agree to a thorough screening by professionals trained in this area. Even if they do not, it is still your responsibility to call your local Early Childhood Intervention agency. With their assistance, you should be able to get the child the services they need. This is a time where your teamwork skills will be crucial. It occasionally happens that a family is unwilling or unable to accept that the child has a delay or a significant challenge and will reject services. If this creates a situation where you cannot serve the child's needs in your program, you may have to take the family off enrollment.

The methods for evaluating a child's development are numerous. When looking at an infant or toddler's development, developmental checklists are the most common tools utilized. An example assessment is provided in the free workbook. Older children can use them, but skill tests are used as well. For instance, you may be checking to see how a child is doing in her fine motor skill development, so a series of skill tests are presented to the child. These might include cutting a three-inch wide strip of paper, pouring milk into a cup, building a tower as high as the table, pedaling a tricycle, and tracing a shape with a drawing tool.

Evaluation may take many forms such as a checklist or an assessment of their portfolio. In any case, you are looking for a continuation on a developmental path or a significant deviation from the norm. Variation above or below the norm should cue you to alter your teaching methods for that child. Ask special needs professionals for assistance in tailoring your program to challenge and meet the child's needs.

Most of the time, the assessment will show normal progression. Frequently taking time to step back from the day-to-day work with a child allows you to see him or her more clearly. Take time to appreciate the progress made and the child's unique talents. Use the child's talents as a springboard for curriculum development for the next semester, month, or year. The evaluation notes will be a great thing to share with the parents. Share the accomplishments as you shared the work of educating and supporting their child.

- Additionally, periodic assessment of the class and the methods being utilized is essential. What skills are in evidence in the class, and what areas need support? Are the rules for guiding behavior appropriate? Are the activities serving the needs of the current group of children? Is the class able to transition from one task to another effectively such as from center time to hand-washing for snack? Are there many disruptions and negative behaviors? Does the class have a pleasant sound most of the time, or are the frequent outbursts of strident voices or conflict?

These types of evaluations can lead to the goals for the curriculum. Each group is different and needs to have various activities and challenges. Some programs schedule teacher in-services a couple of weeks after the beginning of the term; this way, an evaluation of the class and the methods can be performed once the teachers have gotten a chance to know the class. This method of assessment avoids periods of teacher frustration and class malaise.

Inclusion

Inclusion is often used to focus on the process of having children who are developing above or below the normal range in a class with children who are at the normal range. When included children who are not developing as expected and need support do develop more quickly than the norm. Sometimes the same child can be gifted in one area and delayed in another. Any child with special needs will need to have an individual education plan (IEP) or an individual family education plan. This is a road map for your teachers and staff as well as the family as to how to serve the best needs of that child. The parents and professionals serving the child would develop this plan. Following these plans are what inclusion is all about. Children should be placed in the least restrictive environment to meet their needs. So, what does this mean for your program? Do you have to include this child? How do you staff a program with a child that requires special attention? First, accepting children with differences is required by law, but more on that in section 3.

If Albert Einstein's parents tried to enroll him in your program, he would alter the flow, so you must make reasonable accommodations. For example, if Albert wants to talk to the ants on the playground instead of playing with the kids, this is a reasonable accommodation, providing a theoretical physics lab is not a reasonable accommodation. Please note that reasonable accommodation does not mean providing one-on-one care for a child without additional compensation. Luckily, however, most special needs do not require this care level. For example, in most cases Downs

Syndrome, learning disabilities, speech delays, and sensory integration can all be addressed with little change in your program. For more information on common types of conditions you might encounter, refer to our **free workbook.Download at texasdirector.org/workbook.**

Your staff will need training about what this means to their classroom. This is generally free from either the school district or Early Childhood Intervention Vendor (1-800-250-2246).

Also, a quality childcare program should recognize and celebrate the human family's diversity. For some centers, this is very easy because they have a diverse population enrolled. Other programs have a very homogeneous clientele. Everyone is from the same area, of the same ethnicity, and have similar family structures.

Regardless, our job in education is to prepare children to function in the world. The world is full of people who look different from those children. There are families with different family structures. Different cultures are bound to knock into ours, so it is essential to expose the children to these elements. This is perhaps more important than teaching them that a lamb says baa. They will likely see a Rastafarian man at some point in their lives and have to speak with him. They probably won't be carrying on too many conversations with lambs.

Learning through Play

When preschoolers play, they take the initiative: choosing where they want to play, coming up with ideas, and trying them out. However, this doesn't mean that their teachers do nothing but move around and watch. On the contrary, teachers have a crucial role in helping children learn through play.

Teachers set the stage for children's learning by selecting materials they know will engage them and then organizing them effectively in specific interest areas. They provide guidance if children need help and ask questions to spark children's thinking, all while allowing and encouraging them to experience the power of feeling in charge of their learning. In any one play period, your child might choose to work on a puzzle, build a block tower, look through a familiar book, retell the story, and play a game with a friend. When she's free to follow her interests, learning happens naturally.

Take playing with blocks, for example. When your child can:

- Balance one large block on top of another, s/he is learning to control and coordinate small muscles.
- Place blocks of the same size together, s/he is learning to classify and sort objects by size, shape, and function.
- Experiment to see how high s/he can stack blocks until the pile falls, s/he is learning to predict cause-and-effect relationships.
- Judge how many blocks are needed to fill a space, s/he is learning to estimate and use addition and subtraction.

For more information, read Teachers (and Parents) Set the Stage for Learning, and Preschoolers Eagerly Accept the Challenge, by Diane Trister Dodge and Toni S. Bickart

Play IS Learning

When babies play, they learn about themselves and the world around them. Play encourages social growth, language growth, problem-solving, and imagination. From bubble blowing to blocks, from stuffed animals to stacking toys, babies love to learn through play. In fact, we can use play to help deaf or hard-of-hearing babies encounter the language that those with typical hearing experience learn. We can even find ways to expand every-day activities into creative play and ways to support baby's first attempts at exploring fantasy and imagination.

Babies spend lots of awake time exploring the world through play. While to adults, it looks like the baby is "just playing around," the baby is learning so many new skills. For a baby, play is the best time for learning.

What is a baby learning while she mouths a toy or kicks her mobile over and over again? By the end of three months, a baby will make a little game of reaching and swatting at a mobile or hanging object. She discovers how to coordinate her hands and eyes to get it. She learns that she can make the movement happen. These are big discoveries that stimulate her thinking skills. Let's look at some more examples:

What does the baby learn when he realizes, "Oh boy, when I get this off, I can chew on it and play with my toes!"

- The feat of finding his feet! This takes the coordination of the eyes and hands as well as problem-solving.
- A baby's mouth is a "touch center" with lots of nerve endings. Mouthing tells a baby a lot about what he puts in his mouth.

What does the baby learn when she ponders, "How am I gonna get all these toys in the bucket? If I turn it over, can I dump them all out?"

- Hand/eye coordination
- Logical thinking skills as she solves new problems
- Her actions cause things to happen

What does the baby learn when he determines, "If I pull my blanket over me, I bet somebody will play peek-a-boo with me!"

- He can start up games with others
- He can socialize with others
- He can take turns with family members playing "peek," smiling, and laughing
- Conversations are also a game of taking turns, and he is learning to take part in them
- People are there even when he can't see them.

What does the baby learn when she discovers, "Wow, I leaned over and picked this toy up. When I shake it, it makes sounds! I can do it again!"

- Large motor skills
- Balance
- Her actions cause things to happen

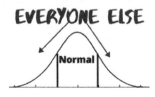

- If she tunes in and listens, she can hear the sounds. This is especially important if she uses hearing aids or has cochlear implants.

Before we end this chapter, let's address two hot-button issues: gender and rough & tumble play. There is far more attention paid to gender now than there has been in decades. Some children are naturally physical and love taking risks. This is often truer for the boys in your center than the girls, but this not universal. It has never been. There have always been girls who are risk-takers: Amelia Earhart, anyone? Some children are more interested in talking and relationships or caretaking. More of these children are female. But if Mr. Rogers taught us nothing else, he taught us that males could be just as concerned with these issues. While biological differences exist between how the normal male and female brains develop, that does not mean those differences are universal. Half of the male and female brains do not fall into the "norm." Therefore, we must make room in our schools to be okay without trying to identify or classify it.

Rough & tumble play is an area in which I can get onto a soapbox, so I will try to limit myself. It will suffice to say that rough & tumble play is essential to proper human development.

Without physical play, chase games, and competition, children cannot fully develop their sense of proxemics (the sense of where your body is in space), empathy, self-control, measuring physical force, or how to overcome adversity. Also, the child must learn that losing is not the worst thing. They must learn how to empathize when a friend is hurt physically or emotionally. We want children who know how hard to push a classmate on the swing without pushing her off. These come from roughhousing. Since this is so important on so many levels, we must help and encourage our teachers to create time and space for these activities.

Branch Out

Spend ten minutes observing a child. Write down what you see in each of the different areas of development.

CHAPTER 11

What Are We Teaching?

"I never teach my pupils. I only attempt to provide the conditions in which they can learn." – Albert Einstein

This central question is key to running any early childhood education and care program. However, I find that it is not asked often enough. Instead, we get wrapped up in what special event we should plan next or what materials to use in the next craft to send home to the parents. Rarely do we actively think about what these activities are actually teaching in our classrooms. This subject came up at a workshop I presented at a Christian childcare conference. We were discussing developmentally appropriate art for holidays versus holy days. Naturally, Easter and Christmas were holy days of great religious importance. Much discussion ensued about what were good age-appropriate crafts to do for those days: the pros and cons of using images of crosses, rabbits, eggs, Christmas trees, and different kinds of stained-glass windows along with which ones could easily be child-directed and which should be teacher-led.

Then I stopped the discussion and asked a question that seemed to dumbfound the entire room: "What are you teaching with these crafts?" No one had an answer. So, I changed the question. "What is the most important message behind Easter at your program? What is the holy message of Easter?" After a little while, this got some answers. The answers included, "It was a miracle," "The tomb was empty," "Jesus rose from his tomb," "Jesus will never die," and "Sins are forgiven." Then I asked how does an egg teach a two-year-old any of those things? Simply put, it doesn't. These activities that they were so focused on were not teaching the intended, important lesson. If the lesson is that the tomb was empty, then a much more useful activity would be to make something called Resurrection bread. If the concept was that Jesus never died or was eternal, then something like an evergreen tree or a perpetual motion machine would be much clearer, more understandable representations to a young child. Whether it is Easter or Ramadan or Yom Kippur or Ridvan, many possible lessons may be taught with any holy day. But we have to identify the core lessons long before selecting the activities we are going to use for that day, that week, or that month. Then and only then should we sit down to design our curriculum.

It's All About Curriculum

Curriculum is an instructive cycle designed to support the children for whom it is being utilized. Curriculum consists of three elements—assessment, goals, and activities—and we can start anywhere within these three and still be successful. We could present activities first, then assess where the child is, and then set our goals. Or set goals for activities and then determine where the children are. Or assess, set goals, and then do activities. It does not matter where we start on the cycle, but we do have to have all three elements to be considered a curriculum. Activity plans are a crucial element of curriculum. In these, we outline specific goals for what we want the children to know or master and then assess whether the children learned what we were teaching. You can develop your own curriculum, buy packaged programs, or blend the two methods. Above all else, the curriculum should be fun, challenging, and developmentally appropriate. If children are not being challenged in some key areas, then the curriculum is not developmentally appropriate. If it does not allow the children a high level of success, the curriculum is also not developmentally appropriate. It's our job to make sure the children have a delightful blend of both comfortable and challenging activities.

Another key element of curriculum is evaluation, and there are two types: a developmental assessment of the child and a review of the environment. After the assessment is complete, that information is then used to create goals which may be either specific to each child or general to the children. These goals lead to the selection of activities.

These form the basis of the planned learning activities. After the children have completed the activities, the adults once again evaluate, recognize what worked well, record the progress, and adjust the goals as needed. Together these elements are a complete curriculum. If a component is left out, the program is unbalanced. If we have not seen where the class or child is developmentally or where we want to support their growth, how can we possibly design lessons for them? To get us started, let's work through one activity plan step-by-step using the four-year-old age group as an example. The curriculum guide provided will serve as our guide. The subject is dinosaurs. Art Given these guidelines and what we know about four-year-olds' fine motor abilities, we will need to have some cutting work, some gluing work, and find a way to word one-on-one correspondence. You might want to have two-person art projects or small group projects to help with their growing friendships.

Art

Monday	Tuesday	Wednesday	Thursday	Friday
Begin work on Chinese style multi-person puppet. • Trace dinosaur stencils	Cut out dinosaur pieces for paper bag puppet. • Assemble puppet	Work more on group puppet. • Make dinosaur costumes for dramatic play center.	Cutting and pasting dinosaurs to match number cards • Work on a group puppet	Parade around in group with puppets • Make collage of favorite dinosaurs

Group

In planning group time, also called circle time or class meeting, you will need to find opportunities to ask open-ended questions and record their words. Again, we need to be aware of their needs and what skills are just over the horizon.

Monday	Tuesday	Wednesday	Thursday	Friday
Introduce subject	Look at show and share objects brought in.	How big do you think they were?	Are dinos scary? (vote & chart)	List as many dinos as they can.
Ask what they know-record & post	Discuss carnivores and herbivores.	Chart answers (have a vote)	Follow up with discussion of why or why not.	Have the students share info one at a time about their favorite
Explain that they don't live anymore, and		Discuss some		

What Children Are Learning	Best Types of Toys
As children enter elementary school, they begin to master the concepts of teamwork, problem-solving, trial and error, strategic planning, and logic. Fine-motor skills and social skills such as turn-taking, cooperation, and rule-setting are also refined. School-age children begin to identify activities they enjoy and excel in, from music to science to sports and art.	Board games, brain teasers, and card games teach kids about rules, working together, and complex thinking. Kids this age enjoy starting collections -- cards, coins, shells, and so on. Educational and creative computer software hones hand-eye coordination and spatial skills but be sure to provide outdoor toys (jump ropes, balls, bikes) to keep kids active, as well as science and art supplies (microscopes, painting sets) to inspire children's creativity.

Fine Motor

Much of what you will be doing in this area for four-year-olds will be in the art center; however, you will also want to introduce manipulatives relevant to the subject or fresh. You cannot always have materials that reflect the subject, but you should rotate the toys to keep interest up.

You can have additional areas in your lesson plans. This was simply an example. Some lesson plans include every center in the classroom and a couple of outdoor use zones. Others stick to four or five centers and group time. Still, others focus on the different play and learning blocks in the schedule. There is no one best way. The best way is the way that supports your teachers in implementing a diverse, inclusive, and enriching set of activities.

Curriculum Needs

The curriculum for each age needs to reflect their needs. All age levels need to address fine motor, large motor, self-image, verbal development, individual goals, creativity, social skills, and cognitive development. These need to be presented simply.

The Ultimate Guide to Learning through Play
By Rory Halperin
Find out which toys can help boost your child's brainpower.

Birth to 6 Months Old

What Children Are Learning	Best Types of Toys
During the first six months of life, babies are using their eyes, ears, feet, hands, fingers, and mouths to explore their environment. As they reach the 6-month mark, they can focus their eyes, respond to different sounds, lift their heads while lying on their stomachs, roll over, and grasp items like rattles and small toys.	It's important to provide infants with playthings that give them a variety of tactile and visual experiences (different textures, colors, and patterns). Mobiles, crib mirrors, activity gyms, rattles, stuffed animals, bath toys, cloth blocks, teethers and cloth or board books all stimulate the senses. Avoid toys that have sharp edges or small pieces or that make loud noises.

6 to 18 Months Old

What Children Are Learning	Best Types of Toys
Gross-motor skills are developing as babies start to hold items, sit up, stand, and eventually walk. Thanks to advanced finger and hand dexterity, they initiate contact with the world around them. Through trial and error, they learn to lift, push, and pull. By the time babies are about 1 1/2 years old, most can understand the concepts of object permanence and cause and effect.	Peek-a-boo discovery toys and hide-and-seek games enforce the concepts of object permanence (the idea that objects and people are still there even if you can't see them); pop-up toys -- like jack-in-the boxes -- and busy boxes demonstrate cause and effect (when I do one thing, something else happens). Soft blocks and dolls, balls, cloth and board books, nesting blocks, and stackers are also good options.

18 Months to 3 Years Old

What Children Are Learning	Best Types of Toys
Toddlers are imaginative and like to mimic what they see in the real world (Mom giving a baby a kiss, Dad cooking). They begin to show preferences and emotional attachments to people and objects. Language skills are developing rapidly, and children are able to conceive complex ideas and thoughts. They are also becoming much more independent (for example, feeding and dressing themselves).	Choose toys like shape sorters, puzzles with knobs, lacing toys, and building blocks to boost hand-eye coordination. Pretend kitchens, tool benches, and other props allow toddlers to imitate adults. Toddlers are very active, so they need toys that let them run, walk, and push (push and pull toys, small wagons, and tricycles). Encourage creativity with an easel and non-toxic art supplies or with everyday items like boxes.

3 to 5 Years Old

What Children Are Learning	Best Types of Toys
Peers become more important as children move from parallel play to group play. Through fantasy and pretend play -- having tea parties and playing store and school -- kids learn about different relationships and roles. Children this age are learning social skills, practicing negotiation, and beginning to understand rules. They are also fine-tuning their art skills. Concentration level and hand-eye coordination also improve.	Dress-up clothes, pretend kitchens, puppet theaters, and other props foster preschoolers' imagination. Simple board games, like Chutes and Ladders and Candy Land, are a great introduction to rules; rhyming, word, and memory games encourage language and cognitive skills. Blocks, train sets, tape players with microphones, and other open-ended toys nurture storytelling and creativity.

5 Years Old and Up

Lesson plans can be laid out in a wide variety of ways. I have added a few for you to explore.

WEEKLY LESSON PLAN

	MON	TUE	WED	THU	FRI
CIRCLE TIME Music & Movement / Book					

	MON	TUE	WED	THU	FRI
LANGUAGE & ARTS					

	MON	TUE	WED	THU	FRI
MATH OR SCIENCE					

	MON	TUE	WED	THU	FRI
MOTOR SKILLS					

	MON	TUE	WED	THU	FRI
SENSORY PLAY					

LESSON PLAN

THEME	NOTES

math	science	reading

sensory	fine motor skills	large motor skills

sharing time	books	music & dance

WEEKLY LESSON PLAN

DATE: UNIT: TOPIC:

LESSON ACTIVITIES

CIRCLE TIME FOCUS & TOOLS	ADULT LED ACTIVITIES	PROJECTS

OBJECTIVES

GOALS ADDRESSED	ASSESSMENT TOOLS

CENTER CHANGES

BLOCKS

DRAMATIC PLAY

MANIPULATIVES/PUZZLES

ART

TEXTURE PLAY

SAMPLE COMPLETED LESSON PLAN
Week of   March 17
Theme   St. Patrick's Day, Green, make Shamrocks
Skills/Concepts to emphasize:
Describe weather using rainy, sunny, calm & windy.
Cutting and tearing paper along designated lines.

Monday	Tuesday	Wednesday	Thursday	Friday
Group time (songs, stories, games)				
Talk about March weather. –check knowledge Number: 14, Alphabet: M I Know My Colors	Introduce new vocabulary about weather St. Patrick's Gold, Lucky, Grass Number: 14	I Know My Colors Mouse Paint Alphabet: M Show and Share	Discuss yesterday's field trip Chart types of grass. Where is Ireland? What was the weather on the walk?	Shamrocks as a luck symbol Mouse Paint St. Patrick's Gold Review of concepts
Special activities				
Make a rainbow Shamrock rubbing	Shamrock headband Shamrock collage	Field trip- Walking around the area looking for clovers	Finger painting with green shaving cream	Shamrock stained glass Video day
Outdoor activities				
Blowing bubbles	Green Playdough	Painting fence with green water	Blowing bubbles	Finger painting with green shaving cream

Evaluation: What worked well?

What should be done differently next time?

Ideas of things to add

Branch Out

Select a lesson plan style and create a lesson plan for one class for a week.

CHAPTER 12

How Do We Make Our Centers Work for Us?

Start building your castles on the rocks, not the sand.

To support our students in developing and learning, we need supplies, materials, and equipment. But which ones? What kinds?

When I opened my first center, it had three classrooms: one for infants, one for toddlers, and one for preschoolers. Not super complicated. Surely, I didn't need that much, right? Think again.

I needed cribs, swings, tables, playground equipment, mats, puzzles, blocks, art supplies, play kitchens, toys, paper, pea gravel, tricycles, changing tables, baby dolls, and so many other things. It took years to collect all of the materials I needed.

Later on, I purchased centers which were already operational and had everything they thought they needed. I disagreed. In fact, I thought they had lots of stuff that really wasn't necessary and were sorely lacking some key items. The number of Happy Meal toys I threw away would boggle the mind. What we need in our centers will be defined by our educational philosophies, our aesthetics, and how we plan to teach and support the children. If we keep in mind our core values when evaluating what is in the center and what to add, we will end up with a school with just what is needed and no more.

For each classroom, think through what the learning goals are. How can you support those inside and outside? For instance, unit blocks are a central element in most preschool classrooms. That is because they teach math concepts, support imaginative play, and both gross motor and fine motor development. texasdirector.org/workbook

Write up the developmental or learning goals for each classroom. Be thorough as possible. This document is what you refer to when you are purchasing additional educational materials or equipment. For example, one of the goals for an infant class is to support them through separation anxiety. So what materials support the infant with this rough developmental milestone? A great tool is a Plexiglas-covered family board with pictures of each child's family. Another possible mechanism is an individual photo book for each infant.

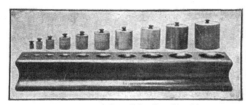

Montessori knobbed cylinders

In a two-year-old class, throwing and hitting is a massive part of their gross motor development. Therefore, materials in the classroom that channel that activity into something safe are essential, such as a hammer table or a drum. Outside, they need balls of various sizes for them to throw.

Fisher-Price Rock & Stack

Children who are working on serration, or learning size gradation, need self-correcting manipulatives to help with that. A classic version is the Fisher-Price Rock & stack. A more advanced version is the Montessori knobbed cylinders.Whether the childcare is provided in a large center or a small center, the quality should be the best possible within the budget. If our purchases are tied to the children's needs instead of what catches the eye in a catalog, we'll go a long way to maintaining a quality program with a sound financial footing. The free workbook has sample classroom equipment lists to help compare and contrast different options.

Beyond the Classrooms

The classrooms aren't the only areas of your center that need to work for us. The office space, reception area (if applicable), isolation area for sick children, kitchen, playground, classrooms, and storage also need to function well.

First impressions are the critical thing to remember:

- What do parents see when they drive by your center? What do parents see when they walk into your center? What do parents see when they walk into a classroom?

Office Space

A simple office with a desk and storage space for files will give a more professional look to and help directors become better organized. This office may also be used for parent conferences and small meetings. It gives the needed place for privacy and even relaxation.

At first glance, this office space tells anyone who enters the room what type of director works there. Are you neat, clean, or scattered? Often, the office is where parents meet you for the first time. This is also where the professionals you work with such as licensing, inspectors, and contractors confer with you.

It is important to organize your office and give yourself the space to work. What areas of your office do you need to spend time on: the files, walls, piles, or shelves? You want your office to have a professional appearance on a limited budget. By accepting donations and shopping quality second-hand stores, you can acquire professional-looking furniture without spending lots of money. If you inherit the office of the former director, a fresh coat of paint and a few new pieces can give a sense of ownership. Take the time to make it your own. To accomplish this, it makes sense to take a bit of uninterrupted time over a weekend. This allows you to put your

personal stamp on the program while not spending much time or money.
Sick Child Isolation

Another element to consider is creating a place for the sick children to be isolated while waiting for parent pickup. The room for isolating children should be a separate room from the other children, but not so far away that the sick child will feel lonely or where supervision is difficult. There needs to be a mat or a cot with a pillow and blankets. In many centers, this is an area of the office or reception space.

Kitchen

The size and type of equipment in the kitchen will depend on several factors:

- Number of children
- Type of program
- Type of food service provided

If you do not serve meals, a small kitchen with a refrigerator/freezer, storage space, utensils, sink, and a microwave will support the serving of proper snacks. If full meals and snacks are prepared, many pieces of equipment are necessary: refrigerator, freezer, stove, oven, sink, microwave, dishwashing equipment, cabinets, cooking equipment, and storage areas. This should be separate from the dining area. Check with the Health Department for additional regulations.

Let's Talk Playgrounds

The location of the playground is key, and this is the part that gets some kids excited. Remember that they will tell their family what they want once they can talk. If you have a great looking playground, they will tell their family that they want to go to your center. There are questions to ask yourself about your playground in the free workbook.

According to the National Program for Playground Safety, there are four key elements to safe play outdoors. These fundamental elements are easy to remember when you know they spell the word S.A.F.E.:

- S–Supervision of children in the outdoor play area
- A- Age-appropriate equipment in the play area
- F–Fall surfacing in the proper depth under equipment over four feet in height
- E- Equipment maintenance

Supervision

Supervision means actively being aware of each child's movements in the play area. It may be necessary to divide the outdoor play space into key regions and assign staff to a specific location. Staff needs to know the expectations of the outdoor supervisor job and the area they have been assigned.

Age-Appropriate Equipment

Although they like to think they do, children from the age of two to five do not have the upper arm strength, handgrip size, and other coordination of school-age children. Equipment in the outdoor play area should be labeled, indicating the age of children for which it is designed to be used. Equipment should be grouped by age, thus enabling school-age children and preschool children to have their own outdoor play area.

Fall Surfacing

The surface used to cover the ground under playground equipment can be a significant factor in reducing the number of injuries children receive while playing on playground equipment. Several different types of surfacing materials are available with varying costs and various advantages and disadvantages. Please see the list of resources at the end of this tip sheet for more information. Wisconsin Group Day Care Licensing Rules require that equipment four feet or more above the ground needs an impact absorbent material at a depth of at least nine inches under it. It is important to maintain the impact absorbent material at the depth required.

Equipment Maintenance

All equipment should be inspected regularly for safety. A checklist of items checked should be completed on a minimum basis of once a week.

Documentation of inspections is a reasonable risk management strategy. A system to address any things that require maintenance and who is responsible for making these changes is also vital. There should be a location to keep the maintenance log on or near your playground(s).

The Importance of Playground Design

Careful planning regarding the layout and design of a playground is another key to promoting safety for children playing out of doors.

Selecting a site

- Consider hazards for children while traveling to the outdoor play area.
- Consider the site's slope and drainage: will the play space retain water?
- Consider traffic hazards and placement of a barrier so that children may not enter traffic areas.
- Choose a barrier material that complies with zoning requirements and allows the children's comfortable visual supervision of children at play.

Locating equipment

- Equipment should be located to separate active play areas from quiet or passive play areas.
- Popular, heavy use equipment should be dispersed throughout the play area to avoid crowding in any one area.
- Equipment should be placed so that a person supervising the playground can clearly see all play space areas.
- Equipment that moves such as swings and merry-go-rounds should be located towards a corner of the playground so that children do not need to pass near this area to reach other equipment.
- Equipment should be placed to clearly separate children of differing ages: all equipment for ages 2-5 is located in one area, and equipment for ages 5-12 is grouped in another area.

- Equipment exits such as slides should be found in a "low traffic" area of the playground.

Signage

- All equipment should have an attached sign indicating the age for which it is intended.
- All signs should be secured in such a way that they are permanent.
- The play area's entrance should bear a sign indicating ownership and hours of use.

What Is a Use Zone?

As defined by the Handbook for Public Playground Safety (available from the U.S. Consumer Product Safety Commission), the use zone is the surface under and around a piece of equipment onto which a child falls or exits from equipment or would be expected to land. This is where protective surfacing or an impact absorbent material needs to be provided. The following information contains recommended use zone standards, as written in the Handbook for Public Playground Safety. The use zone differs according to the type of equipment.

- For stationary equipment (excluding slides), the use zone should extend at least six feet in all directions from the equipment's perimeter.
- For slides, the use zone in front of the access to the slide and the slide's sides should extend a minimum of six feet from the perimeter of the slide. Embankment slides, however, are an exception to this expectation. The use zone in front of the exit of a slide should extend the slide's height plus four feet.
  For Single Axis Swings, because children may attempt to exit a swing while it is still in motion, the use zone in front and in the back of the swing should be twice the swing's height. For example, if the distance from the swing to its pivot (support/hinge) is five feet, then the use zone extends 10 feet in the front of the swing and

ten feet in the swing's back. The use zone also extends six feet on each swing unit's side. Swings should be equipment that stands alone. The distance between the swing seat and the nearest support structure should be at least 30 inches. The seats should be of a soft, flexible material. For preschool children, the pivot points should be less than eight feet above the surface, and the distance from the bottom of an occupied swing seat to the surface below should be no less than 12 inches. The distance from the bottom of an occupied swing seat to the surface below should be no less than 16 inches for school-age children.

Additional Recommended Safety Guidelines

- Elevated Platforms For preschool-age children, platforms more than 20 inches above the ground should have guardrails to prevent unintentional falls.
- For school-age children, platforms more than 30 inches above the ground should have railings to prevent accidental falls.
- For preschool children, platforms more than 30 inches above the ground should have protective barriers. A protective barrier is intended to avoid both inadvertent and deliberate attempts to pass through the barrier.
- For school-age children, platforms more than 48 inches above the ground should always have protective barriers.
- Head Entrapments Hazards Openings closed on all sides should be less than three and one-half inches or greater than nine inches. (Openings between three and one-half inches and nine inches permit a child to enter feet first, but they are too small to allow the head to pass through, improving safety)
- Bike helmets should be removed when playing on playground equipment.
- Hazardous Playground Equipment Animal figure swings are not recommended because their rigid metal framework is heavy and leads to injury risk.

- Free swinging ropes are not recommended because the ropes may fray or otherwise form a loop and present a potential strangulation hazard.
- Swinging dual exercise rings and trapeze bars are generally on long chains and considered athletic equipment items and are not recommended for playgrounds.
- Monkey bars that allow a child to fall onto another section of the equipment is not recommended. There should be nothing except the cushioning materials below the monkey bars.

Children are much more likely to get injured when they are on the playground than in the classroom. Ensure that you have active supervision on the playground and that the playground safety checks are done daily for the basics and monthly to look at maintenance issues.

Now, On to the Classrooms!

An organized classroom results in children who know what is expected of them. It helps your teacher to be able to access needed materials with little fuss and know when they need to request additional supplies. It should facilitate planning the activities for your classroom. That includes the placement of centers. Quiet centers should be near other quiet centers, and art near the water, for easy cleanup. To create a classroom that functions well, you need to:

- Organize the space
- Organize the interest areas
- Organize the specific learning activities
- Organize time schedules and routines
- Organize the people

Encourage your teachers to actively participate in the environmental design of their room. You want them to be comfortable and to feel at home. It should reflect the staff's personalities and students in the classroom.

- You want to foster children's feelings of security and confidence.
- To stimulate children's independence and active learning.
- To enable teachers to work with individuals and groups.

An interest center is an area of the room or yard devoted to a particular learning type.

This may be blocks, dramatic play, large motor skills, music and movement, reading or puzzles and games. Arrange interest centers so that:

- Conditions are appropriate with supplies and equipment nearby the activity. For example, art activities are best located near the sink.
- Children can use the supplies and equipment with maximum independence.
- Toys and supplies are near the area of expedited use and near a surface appropriate for their use.
- The number of seats or lay spaces suggests the number of children suitable for the room and materials and reflects the number an adult can comfortably watch.
- There are clues to appropriate behavior for that space.
- It is in an exciting way that invites participation (open shelves).
- About 50 percent more play spaces than the total number of children in the group.
- Some have both quiet activities and loud activities.

The interest centers should be set up before children arrive. Set up many of them so that the activities can be accomplished independently. Placing similar items together into a labeled container helps organize specific learning activities.

Young children tell time by the sequence of events, not by the clock. They are more secure when they can predict what event happens next. Having an organized daily and weekly schedule helps the children feel comfortable.

The people also need to be organized. This includes the parents and the teachers. The teachers will need to encourage the students' participation to assist with the daily activities when possible. This is using your "manpower" wisely.

The ABC's of Classroom Assessment

This straightforward checklist will help you reflect on the physical space, interactions, and systems that make up your classroom learning environment:

- Accessibility - Materials meant for children are readily available for independent use.
- Balance - there's a balance in spaces and materials between quiet/ loud, big/small, open/closed, soft/rigid, novel/familiar, and group/ individual.
- Choice - Children have opportunities to choose from various activities and materials whenever possible.
- Diversity - The materials, activities, and physical space reflect the children's diversity, including their diverse cultural backgrounds, families, physical and emotional needs.
- Engagement - The environment engages children in many different ways.
- Flexibility - The environment is designed to allow adjustment in materials, learning areas, and daily schedule in response to children's needs.
- Groups - There is adequate space for both whole and smaller group gatherings.
- Humor - Children's humor is incorporated into the learning environment.
- Independence - Children can create their own activities and use learning areas independently.
- Joy - The sheer joy of learning is ever-present.
- Kindness - The physical and social environment encourages children to be considerate of and kind to one another.
- Literacy - Children's language, books, and meaningful print are integrated into activities around the room and throughout the day.

- Memories - Children's experiences are recorded and displayed through drawings, photos, writing, and other creations.
- Nurturing - Children share feelings, sit on laps, receive and give hugs, and have ample one-on-one time with adults.
- Ownership - Children can collaborate to help design and enhance their classrooms. Each child has a place in the room that is uniquely his or hers—a cubby, mailbox, or special shoebox.
- Privacy - The environment allows children to do things alone when they wish to.
- Questions - The environment invites children to ask questions and solve problems.
- Richness - The benefits of a rich and varied curriculum are apparent in the classroom.
- Systems - Management systems and daily routines are built-in, and children have input into rules and classroom systems.
- Time - Children are given more time when they need it to enjoy and get the most out of activities and to complete projects.
- Unity - There is a unifying vision for the environment that includes the perspectives of children and the teacher.
- Voices - Children's voices and opinions are welcomed and encouraged!
- World - Children's outside world is reflected in their classroom.
- eXamination - Teachers continually examine children's needs, adjusting the environment accordingly.
- Yes - There is a positive atmosphere where "yes" is more prevalent than "no."
- Zzzz - There is time and space for rest, relaxation, and, if necessary, sleep.

Questions About Storage

- Do you have enough? What can you use for storage? Where should storage be? What should be in storage? Each class does not need to have all of their glue, construction paper, paint, and other supplies that they will use during the year in their room. Use your resources wisely. This is inventory and should be treated with respect. Do your classrooms have supply budgets? Who buys the supplies? How often? Storage can be shelves on the wall with labeled plastic shoeboxes, a file cabinet, bookshelves, or locked cupboards.

- Out of sight? Easy to find? What is the style and personality of the staff in your classroom? If you like things out of sight, check to see if your teachers work that way before you buy a cupboard. You want your staff to find what they are looking for easily. You want them to be happy with the room and school layout. This is "their" classroom.

Additionally, you need central locations where supplies and equipment not in use in the classroom can be stored. This may range from extra sanitation supplies to wheels for tricycles. Determine where art supplies and other consumables will be stored. Ensure that the staff understands your boundaries on these items. If you buy art supplies once a quarter and they use all the construction paper in the first month, there will be no more construction paper for the next two months. The maintenance and cleaning supplies also need a dedicated storage location.

Location, Location, Location

Yes, the exterior matters. If you have the best teachers, the best classrooms, and bars on your windows, you won't get people in your doors. Your facility needs to be clean, simple, and happy. No need for wild decorations on your building or lots of flowers and plants.

Exterior elements to consider:

- Where is your parking? Where is your signage? Do you have numbers on your building? Can people find you easily? Will they drive by your center and not realize it is a childcare center?

Branch Out

Do a classroom needs list for one class. What are the goals for the children in that class?

CHAPTER 13

How May We Best Manage the Children?

"We should behave to our friends, as we would wish our friends to behave to us. –Aristotle

Now that we have set up our classrooms with the right materials, we add the children... which throws a wrench into things. Picture this. The minute that little Gillian Lynne enters the school in the morning, she heads right for the most visible stage—the largest table in the classroom—climbs up and breaks into song and dance with a massive smile on her face. Now, this might bring a smile to your face as well. I know it would mine. But unfortunately, we can't have the children dancing on the tables all day. As sad as it is, we have to move those little happy feet to the ground.

For the experienced teacher, this isn't that hard. They simply say something along the lines of, "Gillian, please come dance with me on this rug." Gillian then steps down and dances with her teacher. All the teacher did was ask for what she wanted.

This is the core of positive guidance.

Asking For What You Want

A positive approach to guidance focuses on a child's strength and takes a developmental view of behavior. Rather than constantly seeking to control children's behavior or narrowly focusing on inappropriate behavior, positive guidance acknowledges that learning to behave is like any other developmental task a child has to learn. Just as a child needs to learn to walk, a child needs to learn how to behave in a socially acceptable manner. We wouldn't punish a toddler for falling over, nor should we punish a child who makes a behavioral mistake. Mistakes are an opportunity to teach a child a more skillful behavior.

Positive guidance is based on the concept that it is always better to ask for what you want than to tell a child to stop. It does not mean never saying no, nor failing to curb negative behaviors. It involves focusing on the positive: consistently looking at what can be done to generate appropriate behavior.

The aim of guidance is to give children the confidence to take increasing responsibility for their own actions and their effect on other people. To do this, caregivers need to guide rather than control children.

Natural Consequences

Behavior has its consequences, be they positive or negative. We see this every day: the child who refuses to eat breakfast gets hungry before lunch, the child who runs in the classroom falls down, the child who refuses to wear a coat gets cold. These are all considered to be natural consequences of the child's choices.

Since experience is the best teacher, adults may use these consequences to teach self-control. However, it is essential to point out to children that it was their behavior which caused these unfortunate outcomes. Otherwise, children will not learn to take responsibility for their actions. For instance, if left unchecked, the breakfast-skipper may try to blame the teacher for not feeding her on demand, or the injured classroom runner might simply chalk any injury up to bad luck.

Therefore, the best response an adult can make to a child experiencing pain or discomfort due to her or his own actions is to point out sympathetically the relationship between the actions and the outcome of her actions.

For instance, when a child skips breakfast and says she is hungry at 10:30, we reply, "I'm sorry you're hungry. It's because you didn't eat breakfast. I'll remind you tomorrow morning, so you don't get hungry again." Or when a child hurts himself while running in the classroom, we say, "I'm sorry you bumped your head. That can happen when you run inside."

Avoiding Power Struggles

Other than pointing out the relationship between cause and effect, the adult's second role in using natural consequences is to decide when to intervene and when not to. For instance, we can always "make" a child wear a coat when going outside although with some children, this is no easy task. However.by choosing not to intervene—that is, allowing the child to go outside and experience the consequence of getting cold—the child then learns first-hand that wearing a coat is a better choice.

What is most compelling about the decision not to intervene is that the child's "good" behavior—the decision to wear the coat after all—is totally the child's own choice and is no longer the result of a power struggle with an adult. Children are very much like us; they hate being forced to do anything. If they perceive any situation as "I can make you / No, you can't," they will find ways to resist orders and undermine rules at every opportunity. However, when the children are free to make their own choices and learn from experience about the outcome of their behavior, they will become better decision-makers and gain greater self-discipline.

Logical Consequences

Quite often, adults do have to intervene to protect children from dangerous situations or because the child's natural consequence is simply unacceptable. For instance, if a child runs away from the group during a walk around the neighborhood, the natural result is that s/he may be lost, injured, or even killed. The natural consequence of a child throwing sand in the sand center is that other children will get sand in their eyes. Clearly, these situations require adult intervention.

In these cases, the adult's appropriate response is to use logical consequences. A logical consequence can sometimes be confused with punishment because, like a punishment, an adult imposes it due to a child's misbehavior. Rather, it differs from punishment in that:

- A logical consequence is directly related to the child's behavior while punishment is not logically related to the child's action. For instance, it would be inappropriate and illogical to tell a child who ran away from the group that he would not get to play with his favorite truck when he returns to the classroom.
- A logical consequence never damages a child's self-esteem. Responses such as these are more appropriate: "I'm sorry I have to hold on to you, but I'm afraid you might get hit by a car," "I'm sorry you have to leave the sand center, but throwing sand hurts other children. You can come over here and play with playdough for a while."
- A consequence involves prevention and redirection.
- The adult must clarify that the child's behavior has caused the consequence, not the adult.

Now flip-script: what happens if we instead revert to nagging and threatening? "If you pour that water on the floor one more time, I'll..." or "Am I going to have to remove you from the water table?" or "Didn't I tell you not to do that?" The child learns that it is not the behavior that causes her removal from the water table. If it were the behavior, then she would have been removed immediately. Instead, it is now the adult who arbitrarily decides when a consequence is imposed. The adult should not set the amount of time a consequence would last arbitrarily. The child should demonstrate her ability to control her own behavior and thereby bring the consequence to an end.

Understanding Guidance

One of our primary roles as childcare professionals is to help a child create a basic understanding of how the world works. One of the most powerful ways we do this is through our guidance. This guidance is the framework upon which the structure of this understanding rests. Our guidance is a way for children to learn the social rules of our society and that actions have consequences.

All children need guidance. This is one of the few basically undisputed truisms in child education. Without limitations, children have low self-esteem, poor performance, negative self-image, and low achievement in various areas. There is an excellent range of techniques that can fall under the heading of "guidance." For our purposes, we define guidance as tools and methods an adult uses to reinforce desired behavior and detour undesired behavior.

The three basic types of guidance are punishment, indirect guidance, and direct guidance. Punishment is the arbitrary imposition of a negative consequence for an action. Indirect guidance is the guiding of behavior by adjusting the environment. Direct guidance is shaping behavior through direct interaction with a child.

Discipline has very little, if any, place in quality education. Name-calling and bullying are a child's way of internalizing this method of guiding behavior. Use discipline as rarely as possible.

Indirect Guidance

- Indirect guidance is an excellent method of minimizing the amount of work the teacher has to do to keep the classroom functioning well. This is a primary form of guidance in traditional Montessori programs. Balance the number of children and the group's age composition with the staff's number and experience.
- Consideration needs to be given to more than legally required adult/child ratios. Appropriate placement of children balances the caregiver's skills, experience, and the children's developmental needs. Inexperienced or new staffers need to be given time and opportunity to develop skills, confidence, and supportive networks.
- Use routines and rituals to influence behavior.
- Routines help children to feel secure and enable them to predict what will happen next. Through routines, children get to know what to expect and what is expected of them. They gain security from

knowing when things like snack time will occur and can begin to guide their own behavior, reducing the need for adult supervision. This helps the caregiver's and gives the children a sense of control.

- Routines, however, need to be flexible and responsive to individual needs. For example, hungry, tired, restless, or bored children will have difficulty behaving appropriately if their needs go unmet. Similarly, if aspects of the routine are not useful, change them and discuss changes with children.

- Routines get adjusted for all sorts of reasons. Some children do not happily accept changes to their routine; therefore, plenty of warnings and reminders that changes are coming up may be necessary. This will offset distress and allow the children time to adjust and prepare themselves.

- Children who have difficulty remembering routines such as younger children or children with autism, ADHD, developmental delays, learning difficulties, intellectual impairment, or language difficulties may benefit from visual reminders of the routine. Display a picture board with photos of various activities planned for the day in the order they are to occur. Thus, the child has something solid to refer to when they need to know what's going on, allowing for greater independence.

- Picture displays of routines can be done as booklets, pocket photo albums, wall charts, poster boards, or whatever suits your setting and the children in your care. As routines change between days and even during a day, pictures should be moved and replaced. Velcro, Blu-Tack, hooks, or clear pockets are good ideas for attaching photos.

- Having rituals—doing things the same way every day—provides children with a sense of security. This may be very important for some children, particularly those with developmental problems, or even those who simply find their lives at home are unpredictable. For instance, preparing to go outside to play can be made into a ritual: "First, we get our sunscreen on. Then we get our hats. Now we can go out to play." Simple, but the act of repeating the sequence enables children to feel secure and develop greater independence in their actions.

- Have the physical environment provide clues and reminders of appropriate behavior.
- Children can regulate their own behavior more effectively if they know what is expected and appropriate within various areas. Clues as to what is appropriate within a particular area can be indicated by the materials and equipment set out, the pictures on display, or the customary uses made of specific areas. As habits can take time to develop, it may be necessary to keep the same space arrangements for the children to learn what is expected and where.
- Arranging the classroom or play space thoughtfully will help to limit misbehavior. Keep "running lanes" to a minimum by staggering centers. Place centers that might need water near the sink. You should group loud centers such as block play, woodworking, and dramatic play together and quiet centers such as art, reading, and science together.
- Other types of environmental clues to define specific areas can be rugs, hula hoops, fences, or markings on the floor. For instance, using a fence to outline a playing field, a hula hoop to indicate where the Legos® must stay, or use a rug to mark the area for storytime or afternoon tea. Following a discussion of what is expected, such physical clues allow children to be more self-reliant as they won't have to check with adults so often to see if their actions are appropriate or not.
- For some children—especially those who are tense or very active—space issues can be a problem. Children can feel worried about their space being imposed upon, or they may stretch their play so that it invades another's space. Marking appropriate/allotted space may help avoid unnecessary conflicts. For instance, using masking tape on tabletops to define a child's workspace or giving individual trays for sand or water play so children can benefit from parallel play without sharing the materials directly.

- Plan a program that reflects the interests and appropriate to the ages, abilities, and needs of your care children.

- Program planning and preparation of materials is a vital part of indirect guidance. If children are interested and engaged in the experiences and activities offered, they will have little time to misbehave.

- If children are unruly, then one of the first places to look is the richness and appropriateness of the program offered. It is much easier to change the program than to change children.

- Boredom is a significant cause of misbehavior. Suppose activities are too easy or too hard or offered too often. In that case, children lose interest. Or worse, they find other unacceptable or harmful ways to use materials to produce exciting results.

- Pacing activities and expectations to suit individual children will similarly reduce behavioral problems. If an individual child's needs are not addressed, they will often react through their behavior. For instance, two children are in after-school care. One will want to eat and get outside and release the energies pent up throughout the day. The other may have struggled to concentrate and follow directions all day and simply wish to stop being directed about and relax for a while. Expecting that either do other than their needs dictate will result in problems. Arrange activities so they attract interest and invite participation.

- Having material out and ready to go can stimulate children to become involved with little direction from adults required. How you arrange materials can also suggest their appropriate use.

- Arrange materials and equipment so that children can use them with minimum help.

- Children like to feel "big" and independent. Keeping things within children's reach can make self-help easier.

- Store out of sight materials you'd prefer children did not use.

- Only have out in view the materials you are prepared to let children use. Store the rest out of sight so that you don't have to continually retrieve them or enter into discussions about why people can't have them.

- Model appropriate behavior.
- Take time to play in the centers. Through your actions, show the children what is expected in each center. Sit down with them during meals and eat as well. They will watch you and have a better idea of what you require of them.
- Arrange storage for toys and supplies near the area of expected use and near a surface appropriate for their use.
- Children need less guidance when things are well organized. For example, if puzzles are stored near a table, they can be used. Then the habit of playing with puzzles at that table will quickly develop, and the problem of lost pieces will be avoided more easily than if puzzles were carried to other rooms.
- Similarly, the need to caution children and supervise activities is reduced if carried out on suitable surfaces. For instance, anything involving fluids, food, paints, or glues should be done in areas with hard surfaces that can be relatively easily cleaned instead of on carpet. Toys that can scratch wooden floors may be better stored in carpeted areas.
- Equip the room and yard with sufficient play spaces for the number of children in the group.
- It is a simple thing to count the number of possible play spaces to see how many children your room or yard can serve. For example, with two bikes, two swings, and a trampoline, you have five spaces. Indoors you might have the set-up for two at painting, four in the homemaking corner, and three at a puzzle table making nine-play spaces. There should be about fifty percent more spaces than children to provide freedom of choice and suitable alternatives. For 14 children, there should be twenty-one play spaces. Having well-operating equipment that provides adequate play spaces will help keep harmony.
- Another aspect to consider is social space, also referred to as "the territorial imperative" or territoriality. This refers to the area of space around a child that s/he feel belongs to him/her. The amount of social space needed varies with each child. If children experience

a drastic change in their lives such as the birth of a sibling or parent separation, they may feel even less generous about accepting incursions on their space or their possessions. Perceived violation of this space can cause children to feel discomfort and irritation. If they cannot achieve physical distance, they may establish psychological distance from other children, retreating to solitary play with less social interaction (Hildebrand, 1994).

- Caregivers can eliminate many guidance problems by avoiding crowding children in their various activities. If there are frequent behavior problems, caregivers should look into the space and the number of children using it. Reducing the number of children who can be in an area or an activity at the same time may reduce problems.

Direct Guidance

Redirect whenever possible

Redirection simply means to direct a child away from inappropriate behavior and then guide her or him into a more appropriate activity. Redirection only works when there are acceptable and appropriate choices available. For instance, if a child is misbehaving while she is waiting for her turn at the water fountain, you cannot redirect her activity unless you have an appropriate transition activity to offer her instead.

Redirection often means spending enough time with the child to help show her concretely what you expect of her. Redirection and modeling quite often go hand-in-hand. For instance, if you want a child to quit throwing blocks and throw bean bags instead, it may be necessary to take the child by the hand, guide him or her to the bean bag toss, and play bean bag toss with the child for a while.

To recap, quick tips for effective redirection are:

- Active, hands-on participation of the adult
- Specific alternate choices
- Requests for appropriate actions

Catching the Child Being Good

Another way to redirect a child is to "catch the child being good." You do this when you ignore misbehavior and notice only the desired behavior. For example, the teacher calls the children to sit down on the rug for a small group activity. Some children sit, but other children continue to run, wrestle, and carry on. Rather than scold, nag, or reprimand these children, the teacher ignores them entirely and says, *"Joey is sitting down. Lakeesha is waiting patiently. Buddy is sitting down."*

An important distinction needs to be made, though, between this and positive feedback simply intended to manipulate and control behavior. For example, when children are rowdy at circle time and the teacher says, "I like the way Suzie is sitting quietly," simultaneously fifteen little bottoms hit the floor while fifteen little voices cry out, *"Do you like the way I'm sitting quietly?" "How about me?" "How about me?"* Clearly, the teacher used the children's need for approval to control and manipulate their behavior.

On the other hand, if we focus on the outcome of children's behavior beyond mere approval, we will demonstrate respect for the choices children make while helping them learn self-control. In the example of the rowdy behavior at circle time, if instead of stating what she likes, the teacher says, *"Suzie is sitting quietly. She's ready to hear the story now,"* then the teacher shows Suzie that the behavior has positive consequences for her beyond mere approval and invites other children to decide if this is indeed an outcome they would also like to achieve.

By catching some of the children being "good," we provide a concrete example of the desired behavior to the running and wrestling children. As each child makes the appropriate choice, they are acknowledged, and self-esteem is enhanced. Finally, all the children are made aware of their choice's positive social outcome and get to hear a great story.

Using "I" Messages

Sometimes as adults, certain behaviors of children affect us personally. Children who chew with their mouths wide open might make us lose our appetite. Children who talk loudly all day long might give us a headache. Children who use racial slurs might—indeed, should—offend us. It is appropriate in these situations to redirect the child by giving her or him an "I" message, one which explains to the child how her or his behavior affects us. "I *don't want to see a mouthful of peas,*" "*I get a headache when people shout at me,*" "*It hurts my feelings,*" or "*It offends me when I hear those words,*" are all examples of appropriate "I" messages.

It is important to note that none of the "I" messages refer to the child but instead refer only to the behavior. No one, adult or child, takes criticism very gracefully. If we talk about the actions instead of the children personally, then they can change their behavior without feeling bad about themselves or us.

Some adults will frequently use another kind of "I" message: "*I like it... that you put your blocks away, that you're quiet in the hallway, that you asked nicely for the paint.*" Although these kinds of "I" messages do exert a strong influence on behavior, they do not necessarily teach self-control. In fact, behavior aimed at earning an "I like" from the teacher is not much different from earning stars or stickers.

In the long run, the use of the phrase "I like it" teaches children that the only good behavior that matters is that which is noticed and does little to prepare a child for the vast majority of situations in life in which there is no one around to approve or disapprove. ☆

A better way to encourage appropriate behavior is to emphasize outcomes rather than personal approval. For example, if Jamie is quiet in the hallway, we might be tempted to say, "*I like the way Jamie's being quiet*" in hopes that the other children will get quiet, too. However, we can help Jamie learn more about positive outcomes if we say, "*Jamie's being quiet. Now we won't disturb the other classrooms.*" This allows Jamie and the other children see that being quiet in the hallway is a good choice even if the teacher is not there to say, "I like it." ⟶ *Don't use*

Trouble-Shooting Social Conflict

Social conflict among the children generally involves property disputes, acts of aggression, and occasionally, name-calling. Children who scream because someone took their toy, children who hit when they get mad, or who tattle when someone calls them a name need to learn more appropriate ways to resolve their problems.

A common mistake that adults make in these situations is to intervene too quickly and impose solutions, therefore losing valuable opportunities to teach children how to resolve conflict independently.

In the child who screams because his toy was taken by another child, most adults are highly motivated to stop the screaming at all costs. They might remove the toy altogether "until you learn to share," or they might snatch the toy from one child and give it to the one who "had it first." The problem with this approach is that it teaches kids to look to adults for conflict resolution. Therefore, the child who screams when her toy is taken once will surely scream again the next time her toy is taken, secure in the knowledge that an adult will intervene to hand out justice.

Other well-meaning adults might make suggestions such as "Use words" or "Tell him how you feel." These suggestions are on the right track, but they are so vague as to be useless. Use words? What words? Young children don't have a lot of words to choose from.

These kids need concrete strategies modeled by an adult to apply on their own. *"Tell him to give it back"* and *"Ask him if you can have it when he's done"* are good examples of words that we can give to kids to resolve conflicts. *"Let's go play with something else until he's done"* is a good strategy, too. Sometimes the disputed toy becomes less valuable to the owner when the other party either loses interest or just pretends to.

As for learning to share, this is a life-long process that children can begin learning from a concrete model. If the toy in question lends itself to sharing such as a ball or a truck, the adult can say, *"Let's sit down together and roll it back and forth."* If it is a whole set of materials, such as blocks or Legos, the adult can say, *"Would you like to build something with me? Can Joey help, too?"* Once again, redirection works best when the adult is active and helps children get started in more appropriate play.

Children who are hit or pushed need to begin to learn ways to deal with their peers' aggression. When their rights are violated, children need to learn to say, *"Leave me alone!" "Keep your hands to yourself!" "Give it back to me!"* or *"I don't like that!"* rather than always looking to the teacher to protect them, which in real life does not occur very often. Sometimes a simple suggestion like *"Tell him you won't play with him if he hits"* helps children understand that they do not have to be victims, but that they can actively avoid unpleasant situations.

Children who do the hitting and pushing need to be aware that such behavior is unacceptable and hurts other children. They also need to learn different ways to express their anger or get what they want without physical violence. Rather than instantly putting these children in time-out, teachers should practice restraint and patience and help them learn appropriate strategies to express anger or get what they want without hitting. *"Ask Joey if you can have a turn"* or *"Tell Joey you don't like it when he calls you names"* are examples of alternate strategies that children can use when they are angry.

Giving attention to the victim of aggression is an excellent way to show children who may be misbehaving to receive attention that it will not work. Also, the ability to have empathy for others is still emerging in young children, and they often do not really understand that hitting or other physical aggression really hurts others. Therefore, phrases like *"That hurts Joey when you hit!"* tells the child that his or her behavior produces adverse social outcomes and assists in the long slow process of developing empathy for others.

Finally, it is merely an inappropriate expectation to think that young children can share or handle anger and frustration without adult guidance. It is also silly to believe that adults can administer perfect justice. In most cases, adult imposed solutions are arbitrary and aim to end the conflict, not resolving it.

As there is a wide range of techniques that can be termed "guidance," there is also a wide range of efficacy of those techniques. Take time to think about your own experiences and what tools have been most successful for you and the children in your care. You will feel more comfortable with some techniques and very uncomfortable with others. The Power of Observation

Observation is one of your most powerful management tools and the one that directors use often. It can help spot potential trouble, assess situations, and plan for the future.

Observation is the systematic watching and documenting of events. This means documenting what actually happened, not what you felt or how other people felt. Always keep to facts in observations. Focus on times, dates, those involved, what they did, what they said, and noticeable facial expressions. By keeping to the facts, a more accurate picture of what happened is created potential biases are left out of the situation. You can then use this information to formulate your ideas and look for problems.

To recap, things that impede effective observation are:

- Our own preconceptions
- Drawing attention to ourselves
- Using a subjective point of view

After watching a situation unfold, document it promptly. Write down the events within an hour when at all possible. The longer we wait to record our impressions, the less accurate they will be. The other key thing to keep in mind when observing is confidentiality. Your notes may be accessible to others and frequently contain information not meant for public consumption. Therefore, you must institute measures to guard confidentiality. Using initials or pseudonyms on notes helps file the notes appropriately and quickly. Notes pertinent to staff performance should go into confidential files. Notes concerning a child's behavior or development should go in the child's confidential file. Notes about policies should go in a file for staff meetings or other relevant files. Observations about a current concern need to be filed in such a way as to keep the matter fresh in your mind while guarding its confidentiality. To ensuring that all observations are confidential, keep them in a locked drawer when not in use.

To recap, steps to take to protect confidentiality are:

- Only use initials
- Type your observations in a password protected file
- Use nicknames
- Not refer to the child by age

Your observations will generally fall into one of two categories: formal and informal.

Formal Observation

Formal observations are primarily useful for evaluation purposes. In this type of observation, the adults involved generally know when the observation will occur and the broad outlines of the observation goals. In many cases, the staff has received a full copy of the observation criteria. Accreditation validation visits are a prime example of this type of scrutiny.

This procedure is used when preparing for any type of certification, when doing a developmental assessment, screening at the end of the probationary employment period, and verifying that procedures are working correctly. Additional reasons for using this method will occur from time to time.

Informal Observation

You will more frequently be engaging in informal observation: watching what is happening on an on-going basis. This can take the form of leaving your office door open in the morning to see how a teacher handles the greeting with a parent who has had concerns. It can be visiting with a parent in a classroom while watching what else is happening in the room. These events are the lifeblood of your center and making sure that they are happening appropriately is a daily duty. Watching your center's mundane activities also gives you a great way to compliment your staff on what they are doing right and boost morale. The thing to keep in mind with informal observations is that they, too, need to be documented. After you get back in your office (or out of the classroom), take a moment to objectively jot down what you saw. As with the formal observation, you will need to guard confidentiality.

Branch Out

List out 5 ways to use indirect guidance to guide behavior in a kindergarten class.

CHAPTER 14

How Do We Keep the Children Healthy and Safe?

"You can make your children safe in the world, or you can try
to make the world safe for children."

Our primary job in running a childcare program is to keep the children healthy and safe. There is nothing else that is as important. Sometimes unusual or unexpected things happen, and we have to respond to them in the best way possible. A child is swinging on the tire swing, and another child gleefully runs to jump and join his best friend. Being a little too enthusiastic, the second child knocks his friend off. The friend then falls from the swing, breaking her clavicle. There's no sound of a crack. No huge, crying screams of pain. There's just a lack of normal movement, and the child not playing as she usually does. When something like that happens, we need systems in place so that everyone knows what to do. We should certainly have procedures that strive to prevent incidents such as this, but we simply cannot prevent every accident from occurring at our schools. Toddlers will bite. Preschoolers will scrape their legs and arms. Infants will get bruises and bumps. By creating a safe environment, however, we will minimize the number of these adverse outcomes. By having systems in place when they do happen, it's not a surprise to anyone. This allows the negative repercussions to be minimal. To keep children healthy and safe, we have maintenance schedules, procedures, plans, and training. Most pieces of equipment we buy come with manuals which have maintenance schedules included in them. Additionally, once a quarter we should routinely check all the tables, chairs, and other large pieces of equipment to make sure that they don't have any hidden cracks or loose bolts that we were unaware of.

The Importance of Checking for Hazards

Our first priority in providing childcare must be to ensure and enhance the children's health and safety. We do this by being aware of potential dangers and eliminating or minimizing those risks. The two primary types of hazards are *behavioral* and *environmental*. Children spend most of their day inside, and most teaching is done there. Before children enter a room, it should be examined for potential dangers. The critical thing to remember is that what we see at adult height is not what children see. Have teachers get down on their level to spy out potential problems. Children's hands can and will pick up things we would hardly notice and examine them with as many senses as they can. Each issue dealt with is an injury report we are not writing.

Seemingly harmless objects—a pen left uncapped after writing or a bowl of candy left on the coffee table—pose a choking hazard for children. Every year 300 children die from choking on food or other small objects, making it the most common cause of accidental death in children under one's age. All children under the age of four are at high risk for choking injuries, but these incidents are mostly preventable. Be aware of small objects. Everyday household objects also pose a choking threat. Anything smaller than a table-tennis ball is small enough to fit into a child's mouth. The following items have been identified as top household hazards:

- Buttons
- Marbles
- Snaps

- Coins
- Paper clips
- Safety pins
- Earrings and rings
- Pen caps
- Screws

Once we have eliminated risks, we should also be proactive in preparing for bad things to happen. Each room should have a posted evacuation diagram with at least two routes to exit the room and the building in case of an emergency.

Routine Safety Checks

Make safety a habit. Every day ask staff to do playground safety checks before the children go out to play; at the end of the day, a daily safety check. Once a month, have a fire drill. What other things can we do on fire drill day to improve the children's safety and health in our care? This is also an excellent opportunity for the air conditioner or furnace filters to be changed, for checking the thermometers in the refrigerators and freezers, and to performing a temperature check on the hot water heater. If you have fall surfaces on the playground such as pea gravel, bark mulch, shredded tires, or sand, they all need to be at a certain acceptable depth. Since repeated foot traffic wears these levels down, make it a habit to measure the fall surface on your playgrounds often.

In addition to classrooms, other rooms should have monthly safety checks:

- Bathrooms
- Kitchen
- Office
- Hallways
- Reception area
- Multipurpose room
- Cafeteria
- Storage room

The office should be checked for small items that have been left out when parents or teachers came into the office such as coins, throat lozenges, and push pins. Many things might be left out in the office that could be a danger if a young child comes in while we are distracted for a moment. We should all be looking for choking hazards, electrical outlets being overloaded or uncovered, fall or slip risks, and loose rugs. We will check to make sure that any new piece of equipment which may be a tripping hazard has been properly anchored. All of this moves toward keeping the children safe.

Transitions

We also want to have policies in place around the riskiest times of the day. Those times are typically when children are transitioning from one place or activity to another:

- When children arrive at the center
- When they go home at the end of the day
- When they move from the classroom to the playground When they get onto or off of transportation

When children are being picked up at the end of the day, we need a system to ensure that the person who is picking up the child is on the child-approved pick-up list. Protocol should also be in place if the person coming to pick up the child is in some way impaired. Perhaps they have had alcohol or are taking a medication that impedes their functioning. If that happens, steps do the staff take? These types of procedures are an element of your Standard Operating Procedure (SOP) that we will be discussing in the next chapter. This is an essential part of keeping children safe. **Medical Issues**

When enrolling children into our programs, we need to consider policies to make sure that the children are healthy enough to be in care and that they do not have any injuries that we're unaware of. Before a child begins coming to your program, they must have a statement regarding having seen a doctor in the past 12 months and an immunization record (see index for schedule). Exceptions to this rule can be found in Texas Minimum Standards.

Immunizations are essential to protect children from diseases that could kill or cripple them. These diseases have not disappeared. Immunization records should be kept up to date. This can be done during the students' quarterly file check. Questions regarding immunizations should be directed to the local health department. See Appendix for suggested immunizations.

The Medical Form

Every state has its own requirements for this form. This usually includes an immunization record and a special statement such as the one below, signed and dated by a state-licensed physician.

_____ *has no previous history of illnesses and or injuries that would interfere with participating in the school's program. The program includes close contact with others, daily outside play for up to one hour and a daily nap. The child has been examined by me and is both physically and mentally able to participate in the program's program.*

Emergency Authorization Form

Hospitals and doctors need consent before they can treat a patient. In a real emergency in which we need to seek medical help for one of our children, we need to have a form that will authorize treatment. The Policy Statement

A program's policy statement explains its basic, acceptable rules and procedures. This should clearly define both tuition information and sickness policies, specifically:

- If students are sick, they MUST stay home. If students have a fever, they MUST stay home an additional 24 hours.

A critical element of keeping children healthy while at our programs is the exclusion of ill individuals. If someone has an infectious disease, it is crucial to keep them out of your school. For this reason, we should have policies on what's what body temperature would indicate that someone should not come to school, whether employee or child. Additionally, we'll want to address diarrhea, vomiting rashes, and coughing. Our policies depend upon Licensing and Health Department regulations and the culture at your center. If a child or staff person becomes ill while at our centers, we need to have a place to keep them separate from everyone else until they can go home. Frequently, this is simply an area of the office or the teachers' break room. Ensure that that this area has a place to lie down and access a trashcan. It should not be an area where they will be frequently disturbed. If a teacher or child becomes ill with a reportable communicable disease, we must report that infection to our local health authority. We should be able to get a complete list of the reportable conditions in our area from our local health authority. In general, they are highly contagious diseases and diseases that are currently controlled by immunization.

Hygiene

On a daily basis, we keep the children as healthy as possible by maintaining proper hygiene standards. This includes having the children wash their hands routinely before and after eating, after toileting, after coming in from outside, and after wiping their noses. The children are not the only ones who need to wash their hands, of course. The staff should also be washing their hands at all of those aforementioned times. Additionally, team members will have to wash their hands before and after administering first aid.

Another element of keeping our children healthy is to take them outside daily and allow them to have some free play and large motor play outside. They can get plenty of vitamin D and exercise large muscles in ways that are difficult to do inside the classroom. In fact, it is recommended that children have at least 45 minutes in the morning and 45 minutes in the afternoon to play outside each day. To make sure that this can happen, we must communicate clearly with parents about appropriate clothing expectations. Parents must bring clothes for the children that are appropriate to the weather. This may mean rain boots or a second pair of shoes on a rainy day, warm coats during cool weather, or light clothing in hot weather. A wise woman once told me there's no such thing as bad weather, just bad clothing choices.

Food Choices

Another element of keeping the children healthy is nutrition. Feeding the children healthy food throughout the day keeps their immune system fully functional. The snacks and meals should be replete with healthy, fresh foods to the extent possible with some shelf-stable essentials such as crackers or bread. The more diverse the menu, the more vitamins and minerals the children will be ingesting. It is tempting to serve foods that we know children will eat with enthusiasm, but that is not always the best idea. Children need to have exposure to various healthy foods. A diet of nothing but goldfish crackers and Cheerios with the occasional fish stick thrown in is not a well-balanced diet. Interestingly enough, it takes two to ten exposures to a new food for children to really decide whether or not they like it. Many times, their first introduction manifests itself in a disgusted facial expression, but this does not mean you should never serve that food again. Instead, you should reintroduce it in a week or two in a smaller amount so that they can taste a bite as a side dish. Few children dance with joy the first time they ate salad, but I have seen schools where children are served some sort of salad every day, and they eat it right up. It is just a matter of familiarity. Foodservice is actually also a potential revenue source. The federal government has a food reimbursement program for childcare programs similar to the school lunch program at your local public school called Child and Adult Care Food Program (CACFD). The United States Department of Agriculture administers the program through regional sponsors. If your program qualifies, you could be paid to feed the children in your center. The USDA will reimburse a childcare center for a portion of their food costs as long as the center serves meals that meet federal standards. Participating in the CACFP is an easy way to bring in more money without increasing the fees charged to our parents.

These payments, typically referred to as meal reimbursements, are made based on a formula for the number of children you feed at a given mealtimes the reimbursement rate for that meal. The reimbursement rate varies based on several factors, including the type of meal served and income levels of the children. Specifically, there are three different levels of meal reimbursement defined by the USDA:

- Breakfast
- Lunch and dinner/dupper

- Snacks: morning snack, afternoon snack, and evening snack

For example, in the lower 48 states, the highest level of reimbursement for the 2020-21 fiscal year for lunch and dinner was $3.51 per child served. So, if 60 children are served at lunch, we can receive $210.60 for that lunch! In Alaska and Hawaii, the reimbursement is even higher. We would rarely have all children at that highest rate. But if only 20 children were at each level, the reimbursement is still $139. Add breakfast and snacks, multiply this over a month's time, and we are looking at well over $3,197 in lunch reimbursement. That number is hard to ignore. The rates vary based on the income levels of the children. The USDA has defined three different income levels:

- *Free*–The highest level of reimbursement is given to children whose household income is less than 130% of the poverty level.
- *Reduced*–The middle level of reimbursement is given to children whose household income is less than 185% of the poverty level. *Paid / Base / Denied*–The lowest reimbursement level is assigned to all other children.

We must ensure that we take precautions to ensure that the food we serve is free from pathogens and is not a health risk. Food poisoning can be as mild as an upset stomach, resulting in hospitalization or even death. Many of the foods we as adults eat without a second thought are choking hazards to young children. Please give thought to food safety plans and revisit this issue with staff annually.
Some basics to keep in mind in this area are:

- Serve food soon after it is prepared.
- Cook all meat to an internal temperature of at least 140 degrees.
- Thaw frozen foods either in the refrigerator or stove.
- Use separate cutting boards for meat and produce.
- Sanitize food preparation items after each use.
- Wash produce before use.

- Keep refrigerated items cold, at least 40 degrees.

Many choking incidents occur when food is not chewed correctly or is accidentally swallowed whole. Nuts top the list. Many toddlers can't chew foods like nuts and hard candy because these foods require a grinding motion by the rear molar teeth which toddlers don't have yet.

Foods that are naturally round or are cut into round pieces are also dangerous because they lodge easily in the throat. These foods should be cut into small, bite-sized pieces or avoided altogether.

The following foods have been labeled dangerous by the American Academy of Pediatrics and contribute to the most significant number of choking incidents in young children:

Nuts	Hot Dogs	Peanut Butter
Hard Candy	Chunks of Meat	Popcorn
Grapes	Raw Carrots	Apples

Food Allergies

When developing our menus, we must be aware of children's food allergies or intolerances, which should be outlined on their enrollment paperwork. Joni Levine with Child Care Lounge posted the following helpful food allergy information for parents and providers on the About Child Care Forum and agreed to have the information passed along. This is good information to reproduce and include with our enrollment forms:

If your child has food allergies, you may be accustomed to taking the necessary precautions and managing allergic reactions. When your child is in childcare, you will no longer be there to prevent or respond to their food allergies. Your child is too young for you to rely on them to manage their own health; therefore, close communication is key.

1. When possible, select a caregiver that has had training on how to recognize and respond to food allergies.
2. Pack all of your child's meals. Ask the program director or provider not to feed your child anything without your approval

3. Prepare a written emergency treatment plan to be followed if your child has an allergic reaction. You should include a list of all allergens, signs of an allergic reaction, and types and doses of medications to be used. Identify a protocol for an emergency; be sure to include contact information for you and your child's doctor.

4. Ask the childcare program manager to make sure all potential providers are aware of your child's allergies and that they have access to the written emergency treatment plan.

5. Have your child wear a Medic Alert bracelet.

6. Ask your providers to discourage the practice of food sharing. They should be particularly alert during special events such as picnics or parties.

Branch Out

Make a classroom need list for one class. What are the goals for the children in that class?

CHAPTER 15

What Do You Do When the Worst Happens?

Start building your castles on the rocks...Not on the sand.
-The unspoken words

A few years ago, one of the programs we work with was minding its own business when a Hurricane Rita came to town and left it completely decimated. At the time of landfall, the childcare center was full. After the weatherman announced that the center was in its direct path, the center's staff pulled out their standard operating procedures binder and got to work. They called all of the parents to inform them that they would be closing the school early. They called potential alternate locations and verified where they could evacuate children. They knew where they could bring the children in case of flooding or damage from downed trees or power lines. They closed up the classrooms and elevated the wooden furniture. They brought in all loose objects from the playground and stored them in the cafeteria. They packed up all their computer systems and took the backup drives with them when they finally left for the day.

Unfortunately, the weather forecasters were right. Rita came right through where the childcare center had been. Notice I said *had been*. However, because they had systems in place, they could notify their insurance company to use their Business Interruption Insurance to get immediate funds to move the school to an alternate location. Because of the precautions they took, this center was able to reopen its program in less than a week with most of the children that had been at their prior facility. This would not have been possible if they had not had sound systems already in place in their standard operating procedures.

Four Documents to Rule Them All

Well-managed centers have four guiding documents:

- The budget
- The parent handbook
- The staff handbook
- The standard operating procedures manual

All four are needed to have a well-running business. Since we will be talking about budgeting extensively in Section 3, we're going to take time to briefly discuss the remaining three here.

The Parent Handbook

The parent handbook is there to set expectations for the parents. It is not there to cover every possible situation relating to the parents. For instance, the parent handbook should not have a biting policy in it since it's usually not the parents doing the biting. However, the parent handbook should have dispute resolution information: answers to questions such as "How will the center handle it when there is a problematic situation with a parent?" and "Is the parent first to approach the teacher or come to the director?"

The parent handbook also highlights any rules and regulations relevant to the parents' relationship to the staff and childcare center. For instance, in Texas no one may smoke cigarettes or use an e-cigarette anywhere on the childcare center's property, and parents do need to know that. The free workbook is a list of potential topics to cover in your parent handbook.

The Staff Handbook

The staff handbook has a similar function to the parent's handbook. Our employees need to know what the probationary period is for new employment, when annual evaluations are done, how they can prepare themselves for a promotion or a raise, and the grounds for immediate termination. We would also include some information about professionalism and fundamental policies about how to care for the children. However, specific details on routines such as mealtime or toilet training do not belong in the staff handbook. Once again, we have provided a partial list of items to consider in the staff handbook in the workbook .

Standard Operating Procedures Manual

Everything else done in our programs needs to be included in the standard operating procedures. When we first start a standard operating procedure document or binder, it will probably have very little in it. It will have our two handbooks and the procedures we can think of off the top of our heads. For instance, how are classroom supplies ordered? This should be written up and placed inside the standard operating procedures. Over time this will become an extensive manual. The point of a classic operating procedures manual is so that if the organization leaders all got sick with food poisoning at the same time and had to be in the hospital for three days, the center could still continue to function. It explains how morning check-in is done, how staff members ask for the day off, how to notify the groundskeeper that maintenance work needs to be done, and a myriad of other tasks that need to be done throughout your program. The standard operating procedures are a living document. It will never be finished. There will always be something new that comes up that needs to be recorded so that we can be consistent in how we're handling it going forward. There is a list of some of the things that might be in your standard operating procedures in the free workbook.

Branch Out

What are five things that you need a standard operating procedure for at your center?

SECTION III

CHAPTER 16

Who Is the Boss of Me?

"You're not the boss of me!" –Every three-year-old I've ever met

The question of "who's the boss of you" is very important to children. It was very important to my father, too. My father is a linguist. Since linguists study language for a living, my dad was fascinated by that sentence, "You're not the boss of me." He researched and found that there was a similar construction in most European languages. He even wrote papers on it. As a matter of fact, that one sentence is responsible for my getting to go to England, Italy, and Cornwall, following my dad as he spoke at various conferences on this concept.

So, thanks to young children around the world, I embarked on my first international travel. Needless to say, this question brought me a LOT of joy!

Most of the time, the question of who the boss of you actually is does not generate such joy. In our case as directors, it's definitely not joy-inducing. When we ask this, we are considering several things such as *who can get me in trouble? Who can hold my feet to the fire for a slip-up at my center? Who is holding me to a high standard of care and education? Who ensures that my building is safe for the children, staff, and visitors?*

Childcare is one of the most highly regulated industries in the United States. It is because the children cannot speak up for themselves that we are so heavily regulated. Therefore, it is up to others to supervise us to ensure that we are doing right by the children.

Federal Oversight

The U.S. Department of Labor fosters, promotes, and develops the welfare of the wage earners, job seekers, and retirees of the United States; improve working conditions; advance opportunities for profitable employment; and assure work-related benefits and rights. They are the pinnacle of employment regulation oversight. They mandate what employments must be posted at your business, collect all employment data, and prosecute violators of employment law, among other things.

The agency within the Department of Labor with which we all have some familiarity is the **Occupational Safety and Health Administration, or OSHA.** OSHA works with employers to ensure that their employees stay health and safe, just like the name says. The biggest risks in childcare are illness from lack of personal protective equipment and close contact with sick people; back injuries from lifting and carrying things or people weighing more than 10 pounds; injuries to the feet and ankles from walking on uneven surfaces in shoes without proper support and heavy items being dropped; and repetitive stress injuries. Fines for not ensuring your staff are protected start at $5,000 and cannot exceed $70,000 per incident. Requiring staff to wear shoes that protect their feet from falling objects and keep them safe if they have to run across the playground may annoy them, but it is important. OSHA recommends those actively working in the childcare industry wear closed-toed shoes with minimal heel.

The Consumer Product Safety Improvement Act (CPSIA) amended the Consumer Product Safety Act in 2008 and provided Consumer Product Safety Commission with regulatory and enforcement tools as part of amending and enhancing several CPSC statutes, including the Consumer Product Safety Act. The CPSIA included provisions addressing, among other things, lead, toy safety, durable infant or toddler products, and other child products. The agency maintains a publically searchable database of reported dangerous products. The CPSIA defines the term "children's product" and generally requires that children's products:

- Comply with all applicable children's product safety rules
- Be tested for compliance by a CPSC-accepted accredited laboratory, unless subject to an exception
- Have a written Children's Product Certificate that provides evidence of the product's compliance
- Have permanent tracking information affixed to the product and its packaging where practicable

As directors of childcare programs, we are responsible for checking this website, https://www.recalls.gov, for recalled child toys and equipment on a regular basis. Verify that none of these items are present; if necessary, remove them immediately. Also, we should post information about new recalls where parents may see them so that they can ensure the children are safe at home as well.

The Equal Employment Opportunity Commission (EEOC) ensures that all employees have equal opportunity for employment and advancement. They ensure that discrimination in the workplace is corrected and punished. Below are the primary laws over which they have enforcement oversight:

- **Title VII of the Civil Rights Act of 1964 (Title VII)** makes it illegal to discriminate against a person on the basis of race, color, religion, sex, or national origin. The law also protects from retaliation if someone complains about discrimination or participates in an EEOC proceeding such as a discrimination investigation or lawsuit. Under Title VII of the Civil Rights Act of 1964 and various state laws, "'English-only" policies cannot unfavorably affect only employees of a certain race or national origin. Employers adopting an "English-only" rule should ensure that all affected employees are notified about it and about any disciplinary consequences for rule violations. Employers can provide notice in meetings, e-mails, or other written communication. It may be necessary for an employer to provide notice in English and the other languages spoken by employees. More information about language rules, refer to EEOC website.

- **The Pregnancy Discrimination Act** makes it illegal to discriminate against a woman because of pregnancy, childbirth, or a medical condition related to pregnancy or childbirth.
- **The Equal Pay Act of 1963** makes it illegal to pay different wages to men and women if they perform equal work in the same workplace. The law also protects you from retaliation if you complain about discrimination or participate in an EEOC proceeding.
- **Title I of the Americans with Disabilities Act of 1990 (ADA)** makes it illegal to discriminate against a person with a disability in private companies and state and local governments. The law also protects you from retaliation if you complain about discrimination or participate in an EEOC proceeding.

The Americans with Disabilities Act (ADA) protects an individual with a disability, a person who has a physical or mental impairment that substantially limits one or more major life activities; has a record of such an impairment; or is regarded as having such an impairment. A qualified employee, applicant or client with a disability is an individual who (with or without reasonable accommodation) can perform the essential functions of the activities in question. Reasonable accommodation may include but is not limited to:

> » Making existing facilities used by employees readily accessible to and usable to persons with disabilities.
> » Job restructuring, modifying work schedules, reassignment to a vacant position.
> » Acquiring or modifying equipment or devices, adjusting or modifying examinations, training materials or policies and providing qualified readers or interpreters.
> » A public accommodation business is required to make an accommodation to the known disability if it would not impose

an "undue hardship" on the operation of the business. Public accommodation businesses are businesses that are open to the public such as stores and shops, restaurants and bars, service establishments, theaters, hotels, recreation facilities, private museums, and *schools*. Undue hardship is defined as an action requiring significant difficulty or expense when considered in light of factors such as an employer's size, financial resources, and the nature and structure of its operation. A center is not required to lower quality or production standards to make an accommodation, nor is a school obligated to provide personal use items such as glasses or hearing aids.

- **Sections 501 and 505 of the Rehabilitation Act of 1973** makes it illegal to discriminate against a person with a disability in the federal government. The law also protects you from retaliation if you complain about discrimination or participate in an EEOC proceeding (for example, a discrimination investigation or lawsuit).

- **The Age Discrimination in Employment Act of 1967 (ADEA)** protects people who are age 40 or older from discrimination because of age. The law also protects you from retaliation if you complain about discrimination or participate in an EEOC proceeding.

- **Act of 2008 (GINA)** makes it illegal to discriminate against employees or applicants because of genetic information. Genetic information includes information about an individual's genetic tests and the genetic tests of an individual's family members, as well as information about any disease, disorder or condition of an individual's family members (i.e. an individual's family medical history). The law also protects you from retaliation if you complain about discrimination or participate in an EEOC proceeding.

The Office of Child Care supports low-income working families by improving access to affordable, high-quality early care and afterschool programs. OCC administers the Child Care and Development Fund (CCDF), a block grant to state, territory, and tribal governments that provides support for children and their families with paying for childcare that will fit their needs and that will prepare children to succeed in school.

This program funds childcare subsidies throughout the United States. It is administered by a state or regional grantee. In Texas that agency is the Texas Workforce Commission. These subsidies pay centers to provide care for families who are working and/or going to school. These payments are guaranteed by the federal government and can add a level of stability to your income stream.

The Child and Adult Care Food Program (CACFP) is a federal program administered by the USDA that provides reimbursements for nutritious meals and snacks to eligible children and adults who are enrolled for care at participating childcare centers, day care homes, and adult day care centers. CACFP also provides reimbursements for meals served to children and youth participating in afterschool care programs. CACFP has specific guidelines as to what foods can be served to qualify for this program.

There are a couple of laws we haven't discussed yet that are definitely worth mentioning.

The Employee Polygraph Protection Act of 1988 (EPPA) generally prevents employers from using lie detector tests, either for pre-employment screening or during the course of employment, with certain exemptions. Employers generally may not require or request any employee or job applicant to take a lie detector test, or discharge, discipline, or discriminate against an employee or job applicant for refusing to take a test or for exercising other rights under the Act. In addition, employers are required to display the EPPA poster in the workplace for their employees.

Family Medical Leave Act (FMLA) applies to your company if you employ over 50 employees, and at least 50 of your employees work 20 or more workweeks in the current or preceding calendar year. An "eligible" employee allowed leave under the FMLA is an employee that has been employed with your company for at least 1,250 hours during a 12-month period prior to the start of the leave. The 12 months do not need to be consecutive months. The burden is on the employer to show records that the employee has not worked the required 1,250 hours. If the employer cannot show record of work hours, the employee is eligible to use FMLA. In 1990,

Congress passed the **Older Workers Benefit Protection Act (OWBPA)** which amended the **Age Discrimination in Employment Act (ADEA)** to safeguard older workers' employee benefits from age discrimination. Even with the OWBPA amendments, employers may observe the terms of "bona fide employee benefit plans" such as retirement, pension, or insurance plans that contain age-based distinctions, but only if the distinctions are cost-justified. Employers must pay the same amount for each benefit provided to an older worker as is paid for a younger worker. But the OWBPA does make provision for the increased costs of providing certain benefits, such as life insurance, to older workers. The federal agencies have an abundance of resources that you can use to improve your business. Use them as a resource. Sometimes when you are having a hard time getting and employee or client to follow your rules, it can be helpful to cite the federal law that is relevant. Conspicuously absent is the Internal Revenue Service, but don't worry—I didn't forget. We'll address them later.

State Oversight

At the state level are regulations stemming primarily from the designated agency regulating care in your state. There may even be more than one, depending on whether ours is an in-home, out-of-home, out-of-school, or school-based program. A list of the primary childcare licensing agencies for each state is available in the free workbook resources section. Additionally, the state regulates building codes and fire codes as well as employment laws.

It is essential to establish good relationships with our regulatory agencies. They are our partners in providing quality care for children. Since they are focused on health and safety, they may not have insight into educational philosophies. This is okay. We all have our roles to play in this important work. We will talk more about this in the chapter on regulations. Local governments want to ensure the care and safety of their residents. Therefore, they have more specific building codes fire regulations, parking regulations, signage regulations, health codes and general property codes. If you are starting a new program or expanding an existing one, it is important to become familiar with the city zoning and building regulations. How large of a building can you have? What areas of town is a childcare program allowed to operate? How often does your grass need to be mowed? How must your garbage be stored? All of these questions are answered inside your city or county ordinances. A good realtor and contractor can help you navigate these regulations.

Law enforcement officers also have a role in protecting and serving the community. That means that they may come into your program at any time. They may be looking for an individual or responding to a call from someone within the building. If a law enforcement officer is an agent of one of the agencies that has oversees you, they may see any records relating to their area of oversight without needing to get additional authorization. For instance, our health department inspectors may see immunization records or illness reports. However, they may not see employee training files without specific authority because that is not their area of responsibility. In general, police officers may ask for records, but if they do not have a search warrant or similar document, we do not have to produce them.

Outside of all of these government agencies, we also have people who are the boss of us within our own organizations. We may have owners or boards of directors that oversee the operation of our programs. They are there to be a resource to us as much as they are to oversee our work. Utilize them as a resource; ask them questions. Get their help in solving problems. Our in-house bosses are an invaluable tool in operating our businesses.

Branch Out

Take a moment to write down which government agencies oversee your program.

CHAPTER 17

How Do We Organize Chaos?

"We naturally associate democracy...with freedom of action, but freedom of action without freed capacity of thought behind it is only chaos." –
John Dewey

Not only is it important to know who's the boss of you, it's also important to know who you are the boss of. My baby sister is also in the industry. When she was hired on at a new center, she was told that she was going to be the lead teacher in the toddler classroom. She went through her basic orientation with the director and executive director, asked all of her questions, and got her school T-shirt. She was ready to start in her classroom. She introduced herself to her co-worker: "Hi, I'm Lucy. I'm a new teacher in this classroom." Her co-worker said, "Yes, we're co-teachers now."

This confused Lucy. She was told she was hired to be the lead teacher, and she would have an assistant. The person whom she thought was going to be her assistant, however, was under the impression that they were going to be co-teachers. Lucy then went to her director for clarification. "You are absolutely the lead teacher," the director assured her. "You are in charge of this classroom." Feeling more confident, Lucy then asked for the director to inform the other staff member working in the room that Lucy was indeed the lead teacher. The director said she would do this but, in fact, never did. Eventually Lucy got tired of this unnecessary confusion and applied for a promotion elsewhere in the organization. Because the director had been unwilling to clarify the organizational structure or the chain of command or job titles, she lost an excellent classroom teacher. In this case, they were lucky because she did not leave the center all together, but it could have easily gone the other way. And it does go the other way for many programs. Staff members leave centers because they don't understand who is in charge of whom.

Just as a house cannot be built a house without first constructing a frame, we cannot build strong programs without proper structure. This includes a flowchart of who reports to whom, tools for observation and assessment of the staff, and of course, the center's goals.

It also includes knowing what legal structure our center is utilizing. The organizational structure in a large non-profit 501(c) company like the United Way is radically different than a sole proprietorship with one location and an owner-director.

Knowledge of the strengths and weakness of each business structure is important. As the managers of our businesses, it is important to understand the rationale for choosing our particular structure. Because this decision has long-term implications, we as owners should consult with both an accountant and an attorney to help select the form of ownership that is best for our situations. In making this choice, we will want to take into account the following:

- Vision regarding the size and nature of the business
- The level of control. The level of structure to deal with The business's vulnerability to lawsuits Tax implications of the different ownership structures Expected profit or loss of the business Whether or not earnings will need to be reinvested into the business
- The need for access to cash out of the business for the owner

Sole Proprietorships

The vast majority of small businesses start out as sole proprietorships. One person, usually the individual responsible for the day-to-day running of the business, owns is type of firm. Sole proprietors own all the assets of the business and the profits generated by it. As such, they also assume complete responsibility for any of its liabilities or debts. In the eyes of the law and the public, you are one and the same with your business.

- Advantages of a Sole Proprietorship These are the easiest and least expensive form of ownership to organize. Sole proprietors are in complete control, and within the parameters of the law, may make decisions as they see fit.

Sole proprietors receive all income generated by the business to keep or reinvest. Profits from the business flow directly to the owner's personal tax return. The business is easy to dissolve, if desired. Disadvantages of a Sole Proprietorship Sole proprietors have unlimited liability and are legally responsible for all debts against the business. Their business and personal assets are at risk. They may be at a disadvantage in raising funds and are often limited to using funds from personal savings or consumer loans. They may have a hard time attracting high-caliber employees or those that are motivated by the opportunity to own a part of the business. Some employee benefits such as owner's medical insurance premiums are not directly deductible from business income, only partially deductible as an adjustment to income. Partnerships In a partnership, two or more people share ownership of a single business. Like sole proprietorships, the law does not distinguish between the business and its owners. The partners should have a legal agreement that sets forth how decisions will be made, profits will be shared, disputes will be resolved, how future partners will be admitted to the partnership, how partners can be bought out and what steps will be taken to dissolve the partnership when needed, and how much up-front time and capital each will contribute.

Yes, it's hard to think about a breakup when the business is just getting started, but the truth is that many partnerships split up at crisis times. Unless there is a defined process, there may be even greater problems.

Advantages of a Partnership

- Partnerships are relatively easy to establish; however, time should be invested in developing the partnership agreement. With more than one owner, the ability to raise funds may be increased. The profits from the business flow directly through to the partners' personal tax returns. Prospective employees may be attracted to the business if given the incentive to become a partner. The business usually will benefit from partners who have complementary skills. Disadvantages of a Partnership Partners are jointly and individually liable for the actions of the other partners. Profits must be shared with others. Since decisions are shared, disagreements can occur. Some employee benefits are not deductible from business income on tax returns. The partnership may have a limited life; it may end upon the withdrawal or death of a partner. Types of Partnerships That Should Be Considered: General Partnership Partners divide responsibility for management and liability as well as the shares of profit or loss according to their internal agreement. Equal shares are assumed unless there is a written agreement that states differently.

Limited Partnership and Partnership with Limited Liability

- Limited means that most of the partners have limited liability to the extent of their investment as well as limited input regarding management decisions, which generally encourages investors for short-term projects or for investing in capital assets. This form of ownership is not often used for operating retail or service businesses. Forming a limited partnership is more complex and formal than that of a general partnership.

Joint Venture

- While this acts like a general partnership, it is clearly for a limited period of time or a single project. If the partners in a joint venture repeat the activity, they will be recognized as an ongoing partnership and will have to file as such as well as distribute accumulated partnership assets upon dissolution of the entity. Corporations A corporation chartered by the state in which it is headquartered is considered by law to be a unique entity, separate and apart from those who own it. A corporation can be taxed, it can be sued, and it can enter into contractual agreements. The owners of a corporation are its shareholders, and these shareholders elect a board of directors to oversee the major policies and decisions. The corporation has a life of its own and does not dissolve when ownership changes. There are four basic types of corporations: S, C, LLCs and public or non-profit corporations. Advantages of a Corporation Shareholders have limited liability for the corporation's debts or judgments against the corporations. Generally, shareholders can only be held accountable for their investment in stock of the company. However, officers can be held personally liable for their actions such as the failure to withhold and pay employment taxes. Corporations can raise additional funds through the sale of stock. A corporation may deduct the cost of benefits it provides to officers and employees. Can elect S corporation status if certain requirements are met. This election enables company to be taxed similar to a partnership. Disadvantages of a Corporation The process of incorporation requires more time and money than other forms of organization. Corporations are monitored by federal, state and some local agencies, and as a result may have more paperwork to comply with regulations. Incorporating may result in higher overall taxes. Dividends paid to shareholders are not deductible from business income; thus, it can be taxed twice.

S	**C**	**LLC**	**Non→Profit**
→ The choice of smaller corporations	→ Great if you plan to go public or international	→ Flexible, offers liability protection, great for new businesses	→ Allows you to build awareness, and support a cause that matters to you
→ Up to 100 shareholders allowed	→ Unlimited number of shareholders allowed	→ Unlimited number of members allowed	→ No individual ownership
→ Separate legal entity, filing required with the state	→ Separate legal entity, filing required with the state	→ Separate legal entity, filing required with the state	→ Separate legal entity, filing required with the state*
→ Only one level of taxation	→ You have liability protection	→ You have liability protection and tax liability	→ Often no income tax
→ Shareholders must be US citizens	→ Shareholders can buy an interest in the business	→ Allows you to add members to raise money for your business	→ You can raise money for your cause (those contributions can be tax deductible!)
→ The corporation can only have one class of stock	→ Subject to double taxation	→ Not the right choice for companies who plan to go public and/or do business internationally	→ Filing and application fees are higher
→ Not flexible	→ Not flexible	→ Limited admin upkeep	→ Reporting requirements are more substantial
→ Not suitable if you plan to go public or do international business	→ A lot of admin upkeep		→ More admin requirements
→ A lot of admin upkeep	→ Ongoing need to provide additional documentation		
→ Ongoing need to provide additional documentation			

In summary, if you are deciding the form of ownership that best suits your business venture, give the decision careful consideration. Use your key advisers to assist you in the process. If you are working for others who have made this decision, be aware of the challenges this decision presents.

Branch Out

Create an organizational flow chart with all the jobs involved in your program.

CHAPTER 18

Where Did All the Money Go?

"A stitch in time saves nine."
—Proverb

What exactly does it mean that a stitch in time saves nine? It means doing a little something early on can keep you from getting into a big problem later. If you lock down a seam that is loose with one stitch, it can keep the whole garment from falling apart. I chose the proverb because I really can't think of a situation other than financial management where that is truer. Creating a savings account with $5 per week if that's all you can do can save your business in rough times.

At no time has that been clearer than with the recent Covid-19 catastrophe. Some centers had savings accounts. Others were going month-to-month and week-to-week. When the governors shut down childcare in the spring of 2020, the programs that were running without reserves closed... never to reopen again.

Yeah, right, save every month?! Who can do that? I have been there. There are times when putting aside anything into my reserve account seems like rainbows and unicorns. How can I squeeze money out of this already tight budget in order to put some into a savings account that I may or may not ever use? Here's the real brutal answer. **You have to.** You will need that savings account. Your air conditioner is not going to go out in your program when you are fully enrolled and have excess cash. It will go out when you've just lost six families because a new competitor opened in your neighborhood. That is the way Murphy's Law works. There needs to be money in a savings account to pay for that new HVAC system.

There may be weeks where $5 is all that you can put into that Reserve fund. Then do that. Have the discipline to put money away every week. If covid-19 taught us nothing else, it taught us that we never see the unexpected coming. So let's look at how to manage the money coming into your program, , and manage your expenses.

Financial management tools

There are three different financial tools: budget, profit & loss statement & balance sheet. They tell the whole story of your program, from a financial standpoint. If this is causing you anxiety, I want you to know you are not alone. People get very wound up with negative thinking. Have you ever heard any of these gems?

"Oh, that's too complicated for people in a real business." "I don't need those" "Nobody ever taught me how to use those." "They're scary." I just want to help you relax about finances and help you understand how incredibly wonderful they are. You may or may not have had experience with a budget on a personal level. A business budget is a little bit different than a personal budget. One of the things that people tend to think about budgeting is that it is a constraint. Once you have budgeted it you can never make a change. I'm going to challenge you. Just think about it a little differently. Give me a moment put your own personal baggage, your own personal thoughts, about budgeting, to the side and go on a different trip with me. If you got in your car today and decided that you were going to drive to Yellowstone National Park what would you need? What would you want to have in your car before you made that trip? I would want to have a suitcase maybe a tent or maybe enough money to pay for hotel rooms. I would want to make sure that a mechanic had checked out my car. For me that would be a multi-day drive. I would want to tell my friends and family that I was going to be gone for a week and a half. I want to have gas in my car. Perhaps the most important thing I would need is a map or an app on my phone that could give me directions. Is that map a constraint or is it a tool? Can you get from where you are to Yellowstone without some form of map? If you're in the same state and you know general geography you might be able to get there without a map. I live several states away. I know generally which direction I need to go, but I have no idea which highways would take me there. I could get on Interstate 35 and go north but at what point am I going to need to take a left? What is the name of the highway that will take me off of I-35 and out west? I may eventually be able to get there without a map, with just general knowledge and asking questions of people along the way, but it's going to take me a lot more time and I'm going to make a lot more wrong turns. I will probably get lost. So, for my trip to go see the glories of Yellowstone National Park I'm going to prepare myself for success and a great trip by getting some form of map.

That's what a budget is. A budget is just a map. Even with a map I can decide that I want to take a detour on my way to see Yellowstone. I can see a sign for the largest ball of yarn or something and decide that I want to take a detour. I have the map so that after I take the detour, I can get back on track. You have the budget to take you from where you are to where you want to be a month from now or a year from now. It is not a straight jacket. It is not autopilot. It is a guide to making the right decisions based on your end goal. It helps you know whether to turn left or to turn right. Should you buy the new piece of playground equipment, or should you repair it? The budget will tell you.

In many ways having a budget that is well thought-out makes your life much simpler. There are many decisions that you don't have to make. You already know where you're going and if a shiny new opportunity pops up on the horizon, you can look back at your budget and see if that shiny new opportunity takes you in the direction that you decided you wanted to go. If it doesn't take you where you wanted to go, you have a choice to make as to whether you want to go on this detour or not. Will it add too much time to your trip? If it adds another two weeks to my 10-day trip out to Yellowstone I'm not going to do it. If I see a sign on my way to Yellowstone that says turn right to go to Mount Vernon, t it's going to add two weeks to my trip, and I don't have time for that business right now. That might be an interesting trip but I'm trying to get to Yellowstone. If you have an opportunity to open a second location, that's a shiny new object. Does taking that detour get you to your end goal faster or is it a detour? If you have a five-year budget and your 5-year budget shows that you will be profitable in 6 months. That that means that in six months you'll be able to increase your pay as the director or owner. If you open a second center before 6 months you will not be profitable in 6 months. What was your goal? Did you want to have the larger business, or did you want to be profitable? Both are decent goals. You have to know what the goal is so and then create the plan to get there. The plan to get there is the budget.

Developing a budget requires creative decision- making, the ability to look at past business practices and the vision to predict future expenses and income. A budget is written for a specific period of time, typically a year, and is a tool for helping childcare providers predict business success, or in some cases, lack of success. *Some businesses are destined to failure because their expenses outweigh their income.* A good budget will determine success or failure before a provider invests a great outlay of financial and emotional resources. Budget information can also help you make educated decisions about the potential growth of your business. In the childcare industry, staffing will encompass the greatest portion of the budget. Between paying staff wages, payroll taxes, and benefits, there is, frequently, not a great deal of money left to pay for all of the other expenses. If your budget shows more than 45% of your expenses are classroom payroll related, you will have a hard time being profitable. There are several different types of budgets. Each budget generates different information.

BUDGET

A plan for how money will be earned and spent. **START UP BUDGET** A plan for how to get from an idea to a point where a business will break even and begin to support itself. **OPERATING BUDGET**

Projection of what it will cost to operate the business, as well as what the income potential will be.

FISCAL YEAR

A 12-month period of time, which may or may not correspond with the calendar year. This is the year that your budget revolves around.

Since we published a director training manual in 2002, we have found that the SINGLE most stressful and least thought-out part of running a program is the money. Just like in a marriage, failure to communicate clearly about finances leads to divorces between centers and Directors. You need to know what the other decision makers expect. How much tuition needs to come in each week or month. How much money is available for supplies, equipment and staffing gives you freedom. If there isn't any money left in the supplies budget, you can easily say no to that request for 52 new colors of tempera paint. *We recommend that if you do not have a background in accounting that you set up your system with an accountant, bookkeeper or even Quickbooks. Taking a finance class is well worth the money. These tools or contractors will save your wallet and your sanity. It does not mean that you need them EVERY week or EVERY month. It could be annually or when special circumstances arise. We are not talking about your personal taxes or even business income tax. We are discussing business expenses, income and payroll responsibilities.*

We hope that this section will begin to educate and inspire you to learn more about how your program runs and what you can do to save money.

If you are not experienced in managing your personal finances on a budget – do that NOW. It is not a good habit to run your business based on "money in the account." This is called cash flow management and is a sure-fire way to close your business or to increase your stress level. We want you to be able to account for business growth and accounts payable.

In our analogy of the trip to Yellowstone, the profit & loss statements are the landmarks. A P&L tells you how far you have come, the revenue and expenses you have gathered along the way. It tells you about a specific period of time. On this trip, what have you accomplished? We are not looking at your future trip to Thomas Edison's house. We can budget for that. When you're driving to Yellowstone you need to know if you have gotten through Oklahoma. I don't really know how you get to Yellowstone from my home in Austin Texas. I presume you're going north and then you go west but maybe you go west and then you go north. I just don't know. But you have to know when you have gotten to the point where you have to turn. The cash flow statement will tell you when you have gotten to certain goal post. You might use a P&L 5 days after the monthly tuition is due to see where you are. How many parents have paid their tuition? What are your outstanding invoices? That tells you what you need to do next. You see where you are. The Profit loss statement is kind of the mirror image of the budget. Your budget is for a period of time, a month, a year, 5 years. The profit-and-loss statement is also for an amount of time, a month, a year or five years. Your budget is your plan and your profit and loss is what actually happened. The budget is looking out the windshield and the profit-and-loss is looking in the rearview mirror. The profit loss or P&L is also important if you are ever going to need to do things like pay your taxes, apply for a loan or get a mortgage. They will ask for your profit loss statement and your balance sheet when you are applying for a loan. You need to know how to create those and how to read them. An income statement, (otherwise known as a profit and loss statement) is a summary of a company's profit or loss during any one given period of time. The income statement records all revenues for a business during this given period, as well as the operating expenses for the business.

What are income statements used for? You use an income statement to track revenues and expenses so that you can determine the operating performance of your business over a period of time. Small business owners use these statements to find out what areas of their business are over budget or under budget. Specific items that are causing unexpected expenditures can be pinpointed such as; phone, fax, mail, or supply expenses. Income statements can also track dramatic increases in product returns or cost of goods sold as a percentage of sales. They also can be used to determine income tax liability.

It is very important to format an income statement so that it is appropriate to the business being conducted. Income statements are one of the most basic elements required by potential lenders such as banks, investors and vendors. They will use the financial reporting contained therein to determine credit limits.

The last financial tool is called balance sheet. A balance sheet is a snapshot of a business' financial condition at a specific moment in time, usually at the close of an accounting period. A balance sheet is comprised of assets, liabilities and owners' or stockholders' equity. Assets and liabilities are divided into short and long-term obligations. At any given time, assets must equal liabilities plus owners' equity. An asset is anything the business owns that has monetary value. Liabilities are the claims of creditors against the assets of the business.

What is a balance sheet used for?–A balance sheet helps a small business owner quickly get a handle on the financial strength and capabilities of the business. Is the business in a position to expand? Can the business easily handle the normal financial ebbs and flows of revenues and expenses? Or should the business take immediate steps to bolster cash reserves?

Balance sheets can identify and analyze trends, particularly in the area of receivables and payables. Is the receivables cycle lengthening? Can receivables be collected more aggressively? Is some debt uncollectable? Has the business been slowing down payables to forestall an inevitable cash shortage? Balance sheets, along with income statements, are the most basic elements in providing financial reporting to potential lenders such as banks, investors and vendors who are considering how much credit to grant the firm.

The assets and the liabilities are the two elements of a balance sheet. The assets include current assets, (cash, accounts receivable, note receivable, etc.) and long-term or fixed assets, (land, buildings, equipment, machinery, vehicles, etc.). The liabilities and owner's equity are the other half of the picture. These include; accounts payable, loans, accrued payroll and withholding taxes, mortgages, owner's equity, common stock and retained earnings. If you are a director who does not set the budget, you just implement the one someone else created. You need to know what it is because you spend the money. You hire the staff. You schedule the staff. You need to know how the budget is created because a key element of communicating with your superiors is knowing what they are expecting. If the budget says that you have a hundred children paying full-time tuition, but you only have 35 children enrolled and half of those are being funded by federal subsidies, then you know that you're not going to be able to spend the money that was budgeted for new playground equipment. The two sides of the budget are related. By knowing how much revenue they expect you to bring in, and how much they budgeted for payroll supplies and equipment, you know what is expected of you as far as bringing in new clients retaining existing clients and controlling costs. I want you to think of these 3 financial instruments as tools, not as a Boogeyman. These are not the 3 Horsemen of the Apocalypse; they are tools in your toolbox in order to run a program successfully and have the financial success that you want to have in this job.

Revenue streams

The first part of the budget is the fun part of the budget, the income! How do you get money into your program? The first way people have a tendency to think of is full-time care that is paid for with direct payment from the parents. There's also part-time care which can either be Monday, Wednesday, Friday; Tuesday Thursday; or morning/afternoon or school day and then extended care. Most centers focus on these 2 types or revenue- self-pay tuition for full and part-time. Additionally, there is government funded child-care. The largest single payer of childcare tuition in the United States is actually the federal government via the childcare block grant fund. Each state manages this in its own way. For instance, in the state of Texas, the childcare block grant funds are administered by the Texas Workforce Commission which also oversees unemployment and employment law. Research who manages the childcare block grant in your state and what the process is to become a vendor for that agency. I make very few declarative statements in this book about what you must do but this is one: you must have a contract with your childcare block grant agency. You may only ever have one client who needs it. Or you may have 20 or 30% of the people who come to tour your program who need financial assistance. Just because your clients don't need it today doesn't mean they won't need it tomorrow. In some programs it is 90% of their enrollment. It depends on your area and the clientele. Even if you weren't high-end program that is charging top-of-the-line tuition rates I would strongly recommend you have a contract with the childcare block grant agency because you never know when somebody who otherwise fits your parameters might be a graduate student at a local University or have a sudden job loss and have to go through job retraining. In both of these cases they may qualify for the childcare block grant funding and be a good match for your Center, but they cannot afford to pay the tuition on their own. They need some assistance. You may also have employees who qualify, and you can improve their financial situation by having their childcare fees paid by the block grant funds. It is a way to diversify your income stream. We all know the expression don't put all your eggs in one basket. Right now we have two baskets, self-pay full-time and self-pay part-time. I am suggesting, no telling you, you need a third basket of federal childcare subsidies. There may be additional government subsidies in your area. Reach out to your local United Way or other non-governmental family support organization to find out what assistance is available to pay for childcare for families the low-income families or those in emergency situations. They will have information about other organizations that you would want to enter into a relationship with to bring in additional tuition to support families. Some  service those who have children with disabilities or families of government employees. In my area city employees can pay for their childcare before their payroll taxes are taken out, thus reducing their payroll taxes. Then the city has their money to pay for childcare. In order to use that money, they enroll their child at a center that has a contract with the city. I would like to have city employees be able to come to my center. So, I would have a contract with the city.

You can also offer specialized care options. Sick childcare, drop-in care and overnight care are the most common types of specialized diversification. Summer camps are another version of specialized care that programs might adopt.

Another way to bring revenue into your program that we mentioned briefly back when we were talking about health and nutrition is the federal childcare food program (CACFP). If you are a non-profit program, you can automatically qualify for the federal childcare food program. If you are a for-profit program, you may be able to qualify, and many do. This program is based on the household income of your individual clients, so not every program can use this service. The USDA food program reimburses the childcare center for the cost of the food that you were going to serve the children anyway and for administrative expenses. It is not a direct reimbursement. They have set specific amount for each of meal and each category of family income. There are three categories of family income, free, paid, and reduced. It is not your job to decide who goes into which category. There is a form that you give parents at the time of enrollment that they fill out which is very similar to the one that they would fill out when they go to public school for the school lunch program. I have the parents fill this form out and put it inside of a sealed envelope, which I then forward to the person who manages our food program. If you are not a non-profit, then you will need what is called a childcare food program sponsor. That is an agency that acts as a go-between between you and the federal government to collect the data, synthesize it and send it off. Unless you have a 80% of your clientele that are very high-income families, I would strongly suggest that you look into this as an additional income stream.

Other potential income streams include your fees such as annual enrollment or supply, fee field trip fees, etc. You can also generate revenue by renting your facility out on evenings and weekends to aligned organization. Good rental partners include music teachers, lactation specialist, children's martial arts, birthing classes, and photographers. The option the opportunity here is a wide-ranging and is a good way for you to support new business owners & small entrepreneurs. There are also there are other ways to generate revenue such as grants and loans. Grants are generally restricted to non-profit programs. How many other ways can you think of to bring in revenue?

I have not addressed grants. I often get questions about grants to start a childcare program. The simple answer is, don't count on it. If you

operate a non-profit program, then you can find good grants to sup-
port specific programs or purchase equipment. Good grant writers
are expensive and are paid a flat fee for the grant writing before it is
submitted to the funder. If you are any other type of business, you will
rarely qualify for grants.

TIPS ON INCREASING THE UTILIZATION FACTOR

A new childcare center should budget for and try to become 75% full by the end of the first operating year; however, even during the following years the revenue projections will never be for 100%. That would be unrealistic! It is reasonable to hope to be 85–95% full on average, knowing that sometimes enrollment may be higher than at other centers. There are ways to increase or maintain a high utilization factor: Be aware of when there are openings–even part day openings–that can be filled. If there are several openings from 6:00 a.m. until 9:00 a.m., perhaps the center could develop or enhance a before-school program. The school bus may be willing to transport the children to school. *Never develop a program that exists just to fill space and make money. If it's not going to be a good place for children to be, don't do it!* Even when the center is full, continue to market. Remember: the average consumer needs to hear or see about a business three times prior to making an initial contact. This means the business name and logo needs to be out there. Centers that have developed good reputations in their communities are in demand. Parents will call these centers before their baby is born just to be put on a waiting list. The centers then have a list of parents waiting for slots when they become available. It is the center's responsibility to check this list regularly and stay in touch with parents waiting to get their children into the center. There are several tricks to balancing full time and part time schedules for children:

Look for opportunities to match up children with opposing schedules to become full time equivalencies. If a child is scheduled mornings and another is scheduled for afternoons, they fill only one slot as long as they do not overlap. Develop policies for scheduling part-time care, which allow this to happen. Perhaps parents who need half-day care can be scheduled from 6:00 a.m. until noon, or from noon until 6:00 p.m. This allows you to fill empty slots more easily and establishes a clear policy for parents to understand. It is best to limit the amount of part-time care you offer. This helps to keep a steady flow of full-time revenue that can be counted on. Also, part-time childcare is typically priced higher. Think of two cans of tomato paste sitting on the shelf. The larger one costs less per ounce, because it contains more. The shopper who buys the smaller can knows they are paying more per ounce, but they are willing to do it because they only want a small amount. It works the same way with childcare costs. A parent who only needs care on a daily basis may pay a daily rate equal to 1/4 the weekly rate rather than 1/5. *(Example: If the weekly rate for a 4-year-old is $100, then a daily rate might be set at $25/day. If the director can schedule a child on Monday and Wednesday and another child on Tuesday, Thursday and Friday, the revenue for that slot will be $25 x 5 days or $125 for the week. That is more than the weekly rate for a full-time child.)* If part-time enrollment leaves many openings in the enrollment, consider marketing drop-in care, which can help fill the voids.

BREAK-EVEN ANALYSIS

In any business, it is important to know at what point you will "break even" or cover all your costs. In childcare, a break-even analysis is typically done for each classroom, since the child-to-staff ratios are different for each age group. By calculating the break-even point, the business owner will know how many children need to be enrolled in each classroom to cover the costs. In order to calculate the break-even point, first you have to look at the chart of accounts that has been established. Expenses have to be divided into categories:

- **Fixed costs**–those costs that stay the same no matter what the enrollment is (such as rent, director's salary, and repayment of a loan)
- **Variable costs**–those costs that increase as enrollment increases (such as food, toys and supplies)
- **Semi-variable costs**–costs which remain level until enrollment reaches a certain number of children and then increases (such as teaching staff, benefits, and staff training)

- **Revenue**–will increase steadily as enrollment increases

You don't have to do the actual work of creating the profit loss statement, the balance sheet or even the budget. You can hire all of this done. Or you can get software that will help you to do it which is hiring a computer to get it done. To be successful in the long run as a director, you must know how to read financial documents. Working with a good bookkeeper or accountant to learn your numbers is a great way to increase your familiarity. I just wanted to give you the framework as to what those three documents are for. The budget is the guide to where we want to go and it is a visible version of taking your values, your educational philosophy, and putting it into practice. This is where the rubber meets the road. If you say that you value the teacher-child relationships above anything else, then you have to pay your staff well. If you say that the physical environment is the primary teacher of the children, then you have to put your money where your mouth is and buy quality equipment and supplies. The budget is a lie detector. Do you really mean what you say? Are your stated priorities reflected in how you are spending money?

Branch Out

Determine 5 different ways you are going to bring money into your program.

CHAPTER 19

How Do I Manage the Staff?

The most exciting environments, that treated people very well, are also tough as nails. There is no bureaucratic mumbo-jumbo...excellent companies provide two things simultaneously: tough environments and very supportive environments. – Pearl Zhu

I am a huge believer in management by walking around. However, I want it to be very clear with my staff about when I'm walking around managing and when I'm just walking through the building. To make that clear, I had a uniform that I would wear when walking through the building collecting monkeys and seeing what was happening in the present. I put on a jacket with pockets I think blazers are fabulous. Give me a good jacket with pockets any day and I will be a happy lady. You choose your way to let folks know that you are open to taking monkeys. Sometimes when you walk through you just want to see what is going on in the classes. Management by walking around allows you to see what is really happening at your center. The advantage of the pockets is that I could have a post-It note and a put it in my left-hand pocket. That way when I was walking through the program, I could write down things that I saw. If a teacher wanted to give me a monkey, I had a place for them to write it down. I would then take any written post-its and I would put them in my right-hand pocket. When I got back to the office, I could place it on the appropriate page of my notebook. I did this walk through my program twice every day. My staff knew they could count on seeing me twice a day at any campus that I was visiting. When I only had one center, I walked through that Center every day morning and night. When I had multiple centers, I had a schedule. Staff knew when they would see me at a minimum one day a week. I would also stop by at other times so that we didn't have any of that "while the cat is away, the mice will play."

You have to both have the Tiger Time in your office that you defend like a tiger would and time you are managing by walking around. Both parts are important. You cannot manage a staff with nothing but Tiger Time. You also can't manage a business with nothing but walking around and seeing what's happening on the ground. The Tiger time teaches your staff to respect you and your boundaries. The management by walking around allows them to see you as someone who understands what they are going through.

Selecting the team that will work with you to create a professional and positive environment for children is a critical role as a director. There is more to finding staff than getting your friends to work for you. You want to hire "professionals," that are individuals that care about the industry, as well as the children in their care.

Applications, interviews, orientation and training are all a part of the "hiring" process. Staff motivation and continued training will be your responsibility. Training records should be kept up to date. This can be done during the staff quarterly file check. Creating a systems and clear record keeping are vital to staff morale. You want to ensure that you are treating everyone equitably. Having clear systems also makes sure that everyone can tell that you are being fair. You need to be able to answer questions about your students, staff and facility. If you are not there and someone wants to know the answer it needs to be accessible and written down. Keeping records locked away in your head does NO good if you get hit by a BUS. I am once again talking about your Stand Operating Procedures.

At some point you will need to hire more staff. Someone will retire, more, get fired, or quit. You may decide to add a new program. It is going to happen. For many Directors this is intimidating. It's OK. You can do this!

Hiring the right or wrong staff will make the difference. Human resource decisions need to be made with a good look at your budget. The following questions need to be considered:

- What tasks need to be accomplished?
- What skills are required for those tasks?
- How much work will it take for each task?
- How many employees does this amount of work require?
- What financial resources are available?
- How much additional revenue will new employees generate?
- Are current employees fully utilized?
- Are there significant seasonal changes in workflow?
- What new costs will be incurred in addition to salary?
- Will more space be needed? Telecommuting or from home an option?
- Will training be required?
- Who will conduct training?
- Are these needs short or long term?
- Is help needed part or full time?

Just like other aspects of your business, this area can be predicted and anticipated. Growth will prevent stressed out and unproductive staff. Continue to interview applicants once a week or month, even when you think you are fully staffed. You never know when something unexpected will happen.

Before you have your first interview, you'll need to have job descriptions for each of the job titles you have or want to have. Job descriptions are a description of the employee's responsibilities and are designed to benefit everyone. This prevents misunderstandings and makes it easier to recruit, train, promote and provide your staff with career planning.

Again, I can see you cringing. This is not as bad as it sounds. You need a title. What is the job? **Head beekeeper?** OK. Next, we look at the job responsibilities. What does a person do when they have this job? **She supports and supervises the beekeepers in harvesting honey, maintaining the hives, and equipment.** You can be this basic if you want to be. You can be more detailed if you prefer. Bulleted lists work well if you choose go in depth. You should list any special equipment they will have to use. Allow room for adding new projects, a change in emphasis and individual, initiative. The phrase "other duties as assigned by supervisor" can cover a lot of ground.

The next element of the job description is the category. Is this job full or part time? Is it paid hourly or on salary? I think the head beekeeper would be a **fulltime salaried position.**

You are almost done!

Each position needs a list of needed skills, training, experience, or requirements. Our head beekeeper will need to be **over 21 (OSHA rules), have at least 2 years of prior beekeeping experience, familiarity with bee-keeping equipment maintenance and a bee certificate.** The position also needs a pay-range. What is the least you would pay anyone to do this job and what is the most? For this position, **the pay-range is $32,000- $53,000.** (I had no idea) This element of the job description doesn't need to be made public but doing so will increase transparency. There is growing evidence that pay transparency increases employee satisfaction. The last element is where the position fits into the overall organization: who are they the boss of & who bosses them. This also includes what department they are in and what the promotion opportunities are. In our very bee friendly school, the head beekeeper is in **the apiary department, supervises the other bee-keepers and reports to the Director.** Cool! You have a job description. It wasn't super hard, was it?

With a good job description, clear objectives and a sensible plan for hiring the best employees, you can begin the process of finding them. Some small business owners find this task long and hard. Often, they take the first applicant who applies, just to get the task over with. This is NOT the best approach. Instead, you should put your job posting up in places that your ideal client is likely to find it whether that is with employment agencies; in faith organizations or neighborhood bulletins; newspapers; job posting websites; Telling members of your community; reaching out to local schools (counselors can be a gold mine); or ever local workforce commissions. I am old enough to remember the days when most jobs were found in the newspapers. Boy, things have changed!

Applicants: C.Y.A. alert!

Generally, the first contact you have with a potential employee is your job posting. This can take the form of a newspaper advertisement, on-line job posting, listing with a job bank, flier, or a verbal appeal to contacts. In any of these cases it is a good idea to keep some sort of record of the posting. This is helpful in seeing what types of advertising works well to bring in applicants and staff that meet your needs. Additionally, it can provide a record of minimum qualifications required, basic job description, and that you are an equal opportunity employer. **This is to protect you from claims of discrimination.** This is not a specifically mandated type of record keeping, but it is highly recommended that you maintain this information for at least 1 year and longer if you rarely have the need to solicit applicants. The next step is generally receiving an application or résumé. Once you have this material in hand, the person submitting is legally considered an applicant and you and he have a basic legal relationship. You must document that you have conducted yourself appropriately in this relationship. You need to keep all résumés and applications, indefinitely. Any notes that you make based on the application (either your application form or their résumé) that are attached must be kept for the same length of time. If you interview an applicant, your interview <u>notes</u> must also be kept. **Again, this will protect you from any claims of discrimination and refresh your memory as to why an applicant was or was not hired.** If an applicant was considered as a finalist for a position but not hired, when another position becomes available you may wish to contact the applicant to see if s/he might be interested in the new position. If you have your interview notes, you will not have to revisit old ground and can have a more productive second interview.

The job application is a great way to find out information about the person applying for the job. You can buy job applications, use computer templates, or create your own. Protect yourself; paperwork can save you. **The job application must stay in the employee's personnel file.** This form is necessary to:

- Process criminal history checks.
- Make reference check phone calls.
- Contact someone in case of emergency.
- Identify additional needs of your staff.

Warning signs that tell you things are "not right." Look out for these signals and ask questions if you see them. Is it neat and orderly? Does the application look as if the person took time and "cared" about its presentation? Who wrote it? Whenever possible have the application filled out in person. This can let you know the reading level and perhaps the "English" language skills of a prospective staff person. On the go: some people move around a lot. This can be determined by the length of time at their current residence and previous job. The past often repeats itself. Reasons for leaving last job. Look for gaps between jobs. Are they hiding something? Look for patterns. Ask for reasons. Again, the past often repeats itself.

The trend towards receiving applications and/or a résumé online makes it hard to spot some of these red flags. If it has such a major drawback, why are so many using this method? One reason is record keeping. Since applications need to be kept indefinitely, keeping hard copies of thousands of applications a quarter can be quite a large burden. At first, evaluating an applicant based on employment and educational history eliminates many opportunities for prejudicial screening. Making hiring decisions based upon primary characteristics, (race, gender, ethnicity, sexual orientation, etc.) is prohibited by law. It is also bad business practice. If the first round of eliminating ineligible applicants is done in such a fashion, it can make for an equal opportunity workplace. Professional references are very important.

When giving a professional reference you are generally only able to answer questions verifying employment dates, pay rates and eligibility for re-hire. Personal references are not as key in a hiring decision but are still important. They can disclose information that professional ones cannot. Additionally, the applicants' choice about whom to list can also tell the employer quite a lot. Some experience may look and even sound great, remember that different childcare centers have different philosophies. These philosophies can be related to how the business works and/or how children are looked after (re: curriculum vs. babysitting). Additionally, you are looking for other relevant work history. For instance, I have found veterans to make excellent teachers because they are so unflappable.

Interviewing

Before you ask the applicant a single question, you have started to make decision based on their "application" and their first impression. Write these impressions down in an objective way on the interview record for that applicant. The interview record will have the questions you will ask every applicant for the position and leaves room for you to write the applicants answers and the tangents that are part of most interviews. There will be specific questions based on the specifics of each person, but the base questions will be consistent. The general process of the interview will be the same (SOP).

Interview by "10" To make sure that you are not favoring your applicant's, keep a checklist of reminders. These are mine:

1. Handshake
2. Small Talk
3. Explanation
4. Personal background
5. Education history
6. Job history
7. Your questions
8. Describe the position
9. Applicant's questions

10. Close

You are looking for the "one." Someone who presents a positive attitude, smiles, listens attentively, loves being and working with children and fits your center's culture. You don't need 10. You just need 1.

After you have reviewed the applicants, interviewed them and made a decision on the best fit for your organization, you need to make her or him an offer. This will include rate of pay, hours and any benefits (this includes discounted staff tuition and vacation time). At this time, she can ask additional questions concerning your organizations policies. You will need to set up a time to provide orientation and training. You have invested time and money into this person. Make sure they are the best person for your school. Orientation and training

- Once a hiring decision has been made, the applicant has been offered the position and the applicant has accepted the position, you enter into a new relationship, employer and employee. The new hire will need to receive a new employee orientation and fill out additional paperwork. The initial orientation happens before their first day working in the classroom. The initial orientation should include: Going over job description Basic health precautions
- Locations of safety equipment
- Staff handbook or employee manual
- A basic overview of the governing regulations (minimum standards, health regulations, etc.).
- An introduction to key co-workers
- Where to park
- Where to store personal items
- Employment paperwork including tax forms

You will continue to help your new staff member to settle into your program for at least 6 weeks, so they are fully oriented and bonded to your business. Additional elements for orientation will depend upon your program's specific needs. If you are accredited, the requirements of that accreditation will need to be included. If you have an extensive orientation and pre-service training program, it can take place at one sitting or over the span of a few days. As each element is covered have the employee sign that they have been oriented in that area. Just in case you aren't quite sure what all would be good to help your new hire settle in, read on. The clearer the expectations are, the happier everyone will be. Add things a little at a time, so that each team member has time to absorb the information.

Describe your process for determining the hours each employee works every day. Some form of tracking hours is a must. A time clock or sign in sheet are both good approaches. If you have a sign in sheet, make sure to describe the rules about the sheets. Some rules are that no one is ever to fill in another person's time sheet and that all hours are to be kept current.

Find time to go over the forms used for children's record keeping. The employee is shown where they are kept and each form is explained, such as: medication forms, emergency release forms, accident reporting forms and daily attendance forms.

Remember the more the new staff member is familiar with center policies and procedures, the more likely they will be a great staff person.

Give Tour of Building and Introduce to other staff. This is the fun part of the day. As you tour the building, introduce your new staff member to all other staff. Your new staff person wants to belong and not be the "new person".

Your attitude counts. Be friendly as you do this. Make all the people feel important by stating warm qualities they each have as you introduce them.

For example:

"This is Mary. Mary has been here for two years and always smiles and has a positive attitude. Mary, this is Sue. Sue has just completed her training as a Child Care Professional and is excited to be with us."

Discuss the need for team unity. It is important for all the members of your staff to know and understand they are each an important member of the team. They are all working together to create the best possible program. This may mean that sometimes, a staff member has to make some adjustments. He or she may have to fill in for another staff member if needed. They will do this a lot more easily if you, too, are doing your share and filling in. Remember, you are the model for your children and staff.

Explain how children will talk and say just about anything. In a short time, they will provide a lot of personal information about themselves, their parents, and their home time. This information is to be kept strictly confidential unless there is reason to believe that there is an abusive situation. We have the same responsibility as other professionals such as doctors and lawyers. They cannot run around talking to friends about clients and neither can we.

The employee manual covers every expectation and responsibility required by the staff member. This helps the staff member know exactly what you expect and helps the staff member to be successful.

The work schedule is very important. The staff member was hired because he or she was needed. Explain how important it is to be on time and to work the full schedule every day. The children need the stability and routine. Remind them that it is important to be flexible.

Additionally, pre-service training is required of any person new to the childcare field. What this includes will vary based on your state regulations and center needs. This must take place before the employee is scheduled to work in a classroom. A copy of a certificate of training needs to be placed in the employee's personnel file.

The first day on a new job

Unless your interview process includes the entire staff, chances are the new employee will not see familiar faces. You are the connection for that staff person. It is important that whoever is going to welcome the new member of your team be early and ready to greet the new staff person. Make sure they are welcome and that the staff is expecting them.

It is also a good idea to let the parents and children of the classroom know that there will be a new staff person. You are ultimately responsible for the training of this staff person who will affect their behavior with other staff, the children and the parents. Make sure that the goals for the day are clear and set. Just like children, adults want to have a routine and know what to expect. Be careful about additional contents of purses and pockets.

Perfume, makeup and even pills can be poisonous. Make sure that personal items are not where the children can get it.

The Personnel File

What is it? What goes in it? Who has access to it? The confidential personnel file acts as an all-inclusive record of the employee's tenure with your firm. **It includes:**

- Application
- Résumé, if provided
- Annual evaluations
- Other evaluations
- I-9 form
- Criminal history statement and report
- High school diploma or GED, and other education history
- Training certificates for the current year and the one preceding
- Training log
- Conflict resolution forms for the past two years
- Any incident reports for the past two years
- Pay rate history
- Medical information required by your health department or company
- Any other relevant information

This seems like quite a lot of information and it is; however, each piece goes to creating a complete picture of your relationship. The file, as a whole, needs to be kept for three years and ninety days after the last day of employment in Texas. The rules in your area may be different.

The last element of staff record-keeping is attendance. You are required to keep track of the dates and times your staff are scheduled to work, actually do work and the reason given when a staff person does not work a scheduled shift. This information is considered tax related and must be kept for at least three years, but seven is recommended. Motivating and keeping staff

What do staff members want most from their jobs? The key to keeping an employee and to motivating that employee is to know what he or she really wants. Most directors/owners think that what employees want most is MONEY. Most employees think that money is what they want, too. Yet, studies show that this not what they really want at all. They will stay at a job and work hard if their other needs are met. This is what they really want.

1. Full appreciation of work done

First and foremost, employees want to hear that they are appreciated for what they do. Too often what they hear is what they do wrong, not what they do right. Think how good it feels for you to hear often throughout these lessons, "Good job!" Your employees want to hear those words too. A good rule is to never ever let a day go by without finding something to praise about your staff member.

2. Clear expectations

Your employees cannot possibly do a great job if they do not know what their job entails. What does it mean to lead a group of three-year-olds? Be very clear on what you expect from them: total control of the class, children listen and respond to parents, create a curriculum and so on.

Be very clear and include a schedule of what you expect. 8:00 a.m. arrival at work, 8-8:30 a.m. to set up classroom and get out lesson plans, 8:30 a.m. – 9:00 a.m. circle time, 9:00 a.m. – 10:30 a.m. learning centers, 10:30 a.m. – 10:45 a.m. snack time, etc.

3. Feeling of belonging

Your staff wants to feel that they are part of a team and that they "belong there." Each staff member wants to feel that he or she is a vital link to providing what is needed for children in their care and that they are not easily replaced. They want to feel pride in "their" center. They will want to use words like, "we" when they talk about the program. You can promote this feeling of "we" by talking as a "team" and by making each staff member feel important. It's actually the same as creating a family atmosphere. The goal is to have loyalty. You can do this. You must realize that you are a team, and that you cannot play the child care game, which means having a strong powerful center, without a strong and powerful team. It's similar to a football team. You are the coach, the one that inspires your players to make each one feel valuable and that he or she each belongs on the team.

4. Feeling that personal life is important to you – family friendly policies

Each staff member has his or her own life. Some are married, some are single, some have children. They each live in their own unique way outside of work. Staff members want to be able to share a little about this other part of their lives. You do not have to be a therapist. It is more about being a caring human being.

5. Job security

Job security is vitally important. Your employees want to know that their place of employment is stable. It will be there for as long as they want to work there and for as long as you are happy with them. If an employee goes to work for a company and finds out that the company is on the edge, it is frightening to that employee. There is no stability, and then the employee feels, "Why should I put my energy into this organization?"

6. Wages and benefits

This is the area that most employers have always thought was number one. Instead, it is far down on the list. Yet it is still important. It may be impossible for you to give your employees the salaries that they deserve for the hard work that they do. They are the backbone of your center. They are the ones who are "making it happen" for you. You can make it a joy to work for your company. One great benefit is to walk in and see your smile every day because you are genuinely glad to see that person.

When you hire an employee, have a starting salary and then another salary at the end of the probationary period that is higher. Also, have the salary raised each year so the employee knows that something is coming. It doesn't have to be a lot. It just has to be. You can offset the cost through your tuitions. Each fall is a good time to increase your tuition a little – parents expect for prices to increase. You and your employees deserve to get paid more.

Another benefit is discounted tuition for employee's children, health insurance, paid professional days, overtime, and parties.

7. Stimulating work

Your employees want to have work that is interesting and stimulating. They want something to get excited about so that they will want to come to work. You can solve this by giving each employee some responsibility in improving his or her job. One example is to have the lead teacher be in charge of coming up with new themes and decorating their room to match what is being taught.

Everyone needs things to do that are interesting. You would get bored if everything were the same day in and day out. Another example could be something as simple as a new and creative movement exercise to do with the children each day. Encourage your staff to be creative.

8. Example of director

Your staff members need to know that they can count on you. They need to know that you will be loyal, that you can be trusted. You have to set the tone of enthusiasm. You set the tone for being caring, for being loving, for being everything that you want your employees to be. They will be it. They will copy you, their leader. *They need you to believe in yourself and your ability to do a great job.*

9. Pleasant work atmosphere

The actual building has to feel good. It has to be a warm and loving place to come to. Again, you are in charge of creating that wonderful and pleasant atmosphere. The walls, the floors and the noises of the building all contribute to whether it is pleasant or not. We will be talking about how to create the best classroom and building in environmental design. It is up to you to enhance it.

10. Tactful discipline

Employees need to know when they are not doing something right. You are the one who will have to tell them. They will value you more if you can honestly and tactfully tell them what you expect and what is "bugging" you.

Increase Staff Productivity

- As easy as 1, 2, 3...
- Celebrate Staff Birthdays
- Send "Happy Grams"

- Present a fresh flower each week or similar tradition
- Have weekly 15-minute team building meetings. Not your ordinary staff meeting. Use these to acknowledge all the good things that each person has contributed during the week. You can describe how someone handled a parent, a child, a personal problem. Keep the meetings short and informative. This is a great time to have faculty members ask for help with discipline problems, share something new they learned and also acknowledge each other.
- Give an award for employee of the week/month. This is a special employee, even though each employee is special. Everyone has voted in a secret ballet to decide who it is. This is a person who has contributed something especially valuable to the center this week.
- The employee of the week/month gets a badge that says, "I am special" and gets to park in a special place for the week. Even more important is the recognition from peers.

As much as we want to be all sunshine and roses, the truth is that sometimes your employees will mess up. Someone will fudge their time or fail to post the required material. One day you may well be presented with a situation where a teacher does the unthinkable, like leaving a child alone on the playground for a few minutes. Whether you are dealing with a minor issue or a large one, bringing them back to what is expected is you job. If you let one person slip, more will. If you let one teacher break a rule that others are required to follow your staff will start to fracture. That hard won team unity will dissolve.

You have to discipline your staff.

When handling staff discipline, the first step is to find some privacy unless they are placing someone in immediate danger. Provide a safe atmosphere to discuss the situation. Be friendly, but firm. Discuss the problem. Make your expectations clear. Be supportive. Agree on a method to solve the problem. Use the 5 steps of progressive discipline. Follow through with consequences and support. Be tough. Implement the plan. Praise all progress. It is pretty basic. Remember, holding them to account is the respectful thing to do. Letting them slide shows that you don't think they have what it takes. If that is true, then you need to let them find another job where the boss values them.

Progressive discipline

Let the employee know that there is a problem and work together to overcome the problem. Everyone would like to think that discipline is never needed.

Steps 1: Documented verbal reprimand.

Step 2: Written warning in file, having discussed the challenge and the action plan to address the issue.

Step 3: Placement on probation (loss of hours, benefits, and/or last pay increase).

Step 4: Suspension without pay.

Step 5: Termination.

When and if you have to terminate, AKA fire, an employee, you might feel some guilt. It can be hard. Here are ways to get rid of guilt:

- Stay focused and centered on serving your parents and children the best way possible.
- Follow the methods of progressive discipline.
- Be kind to yourself for trying.
- Forgive yourself for not saving the other person.
- Forgive the other person for not being able to live up to the job expectations.
- Know that you're letting the other person be released may be exactly what that person needs for his or her growth.
- Thank yourself for doing your job well.

Branch Out

Write your 5 mandatory interview questions.

CHAPTER 20

Why Do You Buy a Mcdonald's Burger?

If you don't know what you want, avoid what you don't want,
that in itself is a good start. – Lamine Paelheart

McDonald's sells 4,500 burgers every minute, 270,000 every hour, 6.48 million every day. They don't sell that many burgers because they are the best burgers. I've had many a better burger, both in people's houses and in other restaurants both fast service and sit-down restaurants. It doesn't matter that their burgers aren't the best. They sell more burgers than anyone else on the planet. Day in & day out people are making the choice to eat a McDonald's burger when they could go down the street maybe another mile and get a better burger. Why do people buy those burgers?

They buy them because McDonald's is not fast-food store. McDonald's is actually a real estate company with targeted marketing incidentally also sells burgers. What McDonald's does better than any other company in the world, is selecting the right location for their target market. They know where the families and the young adults who are going to want to eat a fast cheap burger. They know where they can sell hundreds of Happy Meals every lunchtime and hundreds more at dinner. They know their Market inside and out. They're not good at making a burger they are good at making marketing and real estate decisions.

Here's the question that you have to answer for you program so that you can be as successful as you can be.

What are you selling and to whom?

This can seem like a big scary deal. Marketing is not what you signed up to do when you took on the job of being a director. You signed up to lead a program. You wanted to support teachers and watch all these children acquire new skills and talents and become amazing people while supporting the family and the community.

Here's the secret: if you don't tell people about how great your program is, you don't get to accomplish any of what you want to do. You have an amazing service to offer. You have a great staff who can bring out the sparkle in a child eye. If you don't tell people about how wonderful your program is none of that matters.

Marketing doesn't have to be your full-time job. It shouldn't be your full-time job. It should take 5 to 10 hours a week in the average program. That may sound like a lot to you, but marketing is not just reaching out to new clients. It's also servicing your existing clients to make them into the raving fans that they should be. Part of marketing is greeting the parents in the morning or saying goodbye to them in the afternoon or taking those phone calls from the parent whose child was hurt. That goes into your 5 to 10 hours of marketing. Remember you're not going to let those be monkeys that run your life you're going to contain the monkeys and keep them to a level that you can handle but that is part of your marketing plan.

In order for you to market, you have to know what you are selling–what is your unique selling position? Your unique selling position (USP) goes back to your educational philosophy. What are your values? Your values and your educational philosophy together with your services and your rates and your programs are what you are selling. When you are marketing you are looking at how can you make an emotional connection to the potential buyer. It's important for you to be able to in 2 minutes or less explain why someone should enroll in your program and not the program down the road. What motivates them to enroll in your program? Spend most of your time talking about your program. For instance, if you know that your program has lower teacher-child ratios then the other program down the road and you think that that is an important quality distinction, instead of saying we have better ratios than ABC Childcare you say we have these ratios it is important to have such low ratios to allow better teacher-child interaction. If your tuition is significantly higher than other programs in your area, you explain during your two-minute speech that you offer a high-quality program where you have the best of X or Y. So, you are overcoming the objection to the price or whatever by framing it to your benefit without discussing the other program. This way you are attracting those parallel parents that we talked about earlier.

The second element of deciding on your marketing plan is to think about the worst family you have ever had. I'm going to challenge you right now to take a moment and really put pen to paper. Write down everything you can think about that one family that you never want to see again, a client that caused you a lot of stress and worry. What did they like about the program? The more you can get clear on what the client's you did not enjoy having, the better you can market to repel them. There are tools for doing this in the workbook. Knowing what they like and what they dislike can help you in your marketing. What they did not like should be something that you consider highlighting in your marketing the things that they did particularly like consider carefully whether or not you want to make that a cornerstone of your marketing message.

Now that you've written about your worst family ever, I want you to write about the ideal customer, the ideal family. We call this your customer Avatar. If you are a visual learner having a graphic image of your best in your worst client can really help you when you're developing your marketing tools. You can name this ideal customer. A very clear description in your writing may be enough for others. What did your ideal customer love about your program or what does your ideal? What media does that customer consume? Are they on Facebook or other social medial platforms or do they just read the newspaper? Where do they get their information, and where do they socialize via social media? What do they like to do outside of parenting? Is there a way that the interest that appeal to your ideal customer can be brought into your program and into your marketing? The better you can get at identifying that client the better you will be at writing the messages to reach that client.

Knowing who they wanted to attract and repel is what propelled McDonalds to be a billion-dollar company. Success leaves clues. Follow those clues and create you ideal customer Avatar. Write down as much as you can about the ideal client: age, gender, type of work, interest and likes. If you need help there are tools in the workbook.

Branch Out

List the 3 things that your worst family likes and 5 things that your Avatar appreciates.

CHAPTER 21

If a Tree Falls...Who Cares?

I would bet that if you are afraid of marketing and sales, then you've already hit a roadblock in your life in other areas. If you don't want to market yourself to other people and sell other people on the value you bring, then you need to look deep inside yourself and figure out why. Maybe you need to work on you, your product, or your service. Regardless of what you want out of life, without attraction and persuasion, nothing works. But it all starts with truly believing in the product and believing in yourself. – Dean Graziosi

If you've got the best program in the world, you have done half of what you need to do. The next task is to figure out how to get the message out to your potential clients. Your local car dealership has their ways of attracting attention. They have those giant dancing blow-up dolls, I think they're called The Noodle, dance in front of the car dealership. They have TV commercials. They have sales on every possible holiday. They place one dealership after another on busy streets, so that all of the potential clients are going to go to that area to look for a car. Now, if they put that giant blow-up noodle guy in the middle of the forest and they ran all their commercials in the next town over would that be helpful? If all the car dealerships in town except one were on one street and the other car dealership was on the other side of town, what is that dealership's chance of success? There has to be a very good reason that the one car dealership is separating himself itself from all the others. Why would someone drive out of their way to go to that dealership? If there are three Honda dealerships in town and two of them are on that main car strip and the other one is across town, why would anyone go to the one that's not on new car drive? You have to know where your ideal clients are going to be. Childcare is what is known as a convenience business for the most part. Most childcare centers are within 2 miles of either the parents' work or home. It's like the grocery store. They choose the one that they can get the services they need to that is convenient. So, your Center needs to be either near people's work or home.

Some centers *are* the destination businesses. A destination business is like an amusement park; people go out of their way to go to that. Childcare programs that offer a significantly different type of childcare are destination businesses. For instance, if your program is a 4-language immersion program, that is a destination type of childcare business.

The key element to keep in mind as you're reading through this chapter is that you must *always* be marketing. Every month money should be going into your marketing budget. It is the last item you should cut from your budget. If things are tight financially, cut back on staffing, equipment, supplies, or food before you would cut back on marketing. If you are not reaching out to your ideal client when times are tough, they will not be able to find you. You will not be able to increase your enrollment if you are not spending money on marketing.

By knowing where your clients are, physically, you can create marketing materials to reach them where they are. You can mail things to their house, have yard signs, have billboards. All of those are methods to reach people where they physically are. You could also try to reach them where they are online or where they are emotionally. If most of your clients are using a specific social media, you need to figure out how to use that social media platform. If most of your clients listen to a specific radio station, you might want to consider what you can do to partner with them on that social media stay on that radio station. There are two types of marketing there is advertising and publicity. They are very different. They are both useful to your business. So, let's talk a little bit about each of those two types of marketing.

Advertising is something that you create and put out into the world. In advertising you control the message, the look and the timing. For instance, postcards are a form of advertising. The signage on your building is a type of advertising. You've seen ads all your life in magazines, on TV, listened to them on the radio. Advertising has its place, and it is important. It is also much more expensive than the alternative, which is publicity. When you are using advertising, you should track who enrolled at your program based on that marketing. If the marketing is not paying off in new clients, then you should discontinue it and find other avenues to try to reach your clients. It takes between 6 and 9 times for someone to see your advertising message before they're going to contact you. So, if you are placing an ad in a targeted print publication or email publication like a neighborhood news-letter, give it several months to see if that actually generates call tours and enrollments. When we are talking about marketing, it is important to not forget about your existing clients. It is much easier to keep a client satisfied than it is to enroll a new one. Hosting special events like family dinner in or a preschool prom make your clients feel like they are part of something special. Creating special mementoes in each classroom a few times during the year also helps bond the families to your program. If parents look forward to when their child is 2 and will be in the wagon pared for Independence Day or 4 years old so they will get to go to a pumpkin patch, they are likely to stay with your program. Building your sense of community and creating memorable experiences are part of your marketing plan.

The publisher, reporter or producer, who is not you, controls publicity. If you are interviewed on the local TV channel, that is amazing marketing for your program. However, it is important to keep in mind that they will interview you for 10 or 15 minutes and only play at most a minute of your conversation. They will edit what you have given them to fit the narrative that they are planning to create. Getting featured in the newspaper it's amazing. People are more likely to believe the messages they receive from media other than ads. There is a good chance you will get inquiries at your program after something big like an evening news segment. Pursuing Publicity takes time and effort. If you have more available time than funds to spend on advertising, then publicity is the way to go. Go out and give talks, get featured in the news, write blog posts, be a guest on relevant podcasts. These can all garner you a lot of attention without spending much money. Both Kate and Carrie have used this method to great effect. The key element to remember is that you should have a goal before entering into a publicity campaign and a metrics to measure to see if it is working. The most powerful form of publicity is actually the word-of-mouth marketing of your existing clientele. Making your current clients raving fans ensures that you will have more publicity in the community. So, the advertising money you spent marketing to your existing clientele can result in positive publicity because those parents are so happy that they tell everybody about your program. Happy Clients Generate Referrals and Repeats.

If you make a promise, keep it. Regardless of Cost! If for some reason you cannot make good on your promise, let the client know AS SOON AS POSSIBLE.

- Answer phones promptly. No more than 3 rings.
- Don't make people WAIT.
- Communicate. Assume the client knows nothing.
- Encourage honest feedback.
- Sell only what the client needs.

Whether you're using publicity or advertising you can do this on a shoestring budget or on a more robust budget. The key is to track what is working and what is not. What is working...keep doing it. What is not let...it go.

PLAN FOR SUCCESS

You have a service to sell. You want to get your program's name established within your market. Where do you start?

Every good idea needs a strong plan of action to support it and make it work. A well thought out marketing plan can help put things in perspective and serve as a guide to achieve your goals.

Here are key steps for developing your market plan:

1. **RESEARCH** is a necessary preliminary step. Know your market by knowing as much as you can about your customer and your competitors.
2. Establish your **GOAL**, a one-to-two sentence statement defining what you want to accomplish. Be specific (how much, in what time period, at what percentage of profit, etc.).
3. Develop a **POSITIONING STATEMENT** that defines your niche and explains how you will position your product or service within your marketplace. Avoid words like quality, service and competitively priced. Those are everyone else's lines. Instead, create something that is memorable and has the ability to break through the clutter.
4. **OBJECTIVE** for the marketing plan. Explain the action needed to obtain your goal, or what obstacles you need to overcome in order to achieve success. It might be things like: expanding market share, a new location, a new service, a better image, or more market recognition.
5. Define your **TARGET MARKET.** Who is your customer? Analyze your marketplace geographically, demographically, socio-economically and any other way possible to pinpoint your ultimate buyer. Highlight primary audiences; those who actually make the purchasing decision and secondary audiences; those who influence the decision to buy your service.
6. List your program's **STRENGTHS AND WEAKNESSES.** Weigh your strengths against those of your competitors to uncover your competitive advantages. Analyze your weaknesses to determine where you may fall short and vulnerable to your competition. Identify weaknesses that need to become strengths.
7. Plan your **STRATEGIES.** These are broad ideas relating to your objectives. Your strategies represent a "big picture view" of how

you are going to address each objective to reach your goal. If you've taken the time to complete steps one through six, the strategies will automatically begin to take shape.

8. Define your **TACTICS** from the strategies. These are step-by-step approaches based on your strategies, highlighting the specific tasks needed to accomplish each objective.

9. A **TIMELINE** is an implementation calendar to match your tactical plan of action steps; prioritizing them first quarterly, then monthly.

10. No marketing plan is complete without a **BUDGET** that defines all costs involved in implementation. Your budget can be based on a percent of sales, (usually somewhere between 1% and 10%) or the task method where you identify the necessary tasks and determine priorities.

11. **TRACKING** will help you to determine which tactics are working and which are not. Survey calls, traffic counts, percentage of sales increases, and number of inquiries, are some of the common forms of tracking. What you may discover from tracking your results is that your method of marketing made the phone ring, but perhaps your enrollment suffered because your staff couldn't answer the phone professionally or return calls or answer the phone at all. **EVALUATION** defines performance milestones and measurement guidelines to determine the degree of your plan's success monthly or quarterly.

A marketing plan is the key to successfully growing your program. Take yourself away from your day-to-day environment and spend four to eight hours of quality time planning. It will pay off!

Shoestring Marketing, the basics–Establishing Credibility So That Parents Take Notice

Demonstrate your credibility through testimonials and community involvement. You can use your current or former clients' testimonials in your marketing pieces, as part of your publicity campaign, and in your advertising. Community involvement gets you high visibility with low liability. You receive exposure and inquiries spending very little time and money. If potential clients see others in the community working with you, you are immediately seen as reliable. Reliability is one of the key elements parents are looking for in childcare.

Showcase your credentials and those of your staff. This positions you as the professional you are. If all of your teachers have CDAs or degrees, make sure everyone know it. Publicize how much annual training your staff member attend. Parents are often blown away by the number of hours of professional training ECE teachers must get each year. You can further highlight your professionalism by publishing and/or through public speaking. You know more about the early years than the average person. Giving a 15-minute talk on how to help a fussy child to fall asleep at a local Rotary club will blow people's minds. If you are more of a writer, you can put fingers to keys and write up that same information and publish it as a newsletter article, a blog post, or even a small eBook.

Remember, marketing takes time. It takes many times seeing your name before someone decides to ask about your services. A good rule of thumb is that it takes 7-12 times to see or hear you before they take their first action. Be patient. The more word of mouth you can generate, the better your business will be. People need to be talking about you. That means if you want to enroll new families in June, you can't start marketing in June. You need to start in March. Give it time to work!

Now for a list of marketing ideas that don't cost a lot of time or money. Decide which 2-3 you will use first.

- Get to know area schools, non-profits, churches
- Enrichment programs – languages, karate, art classes, science clubs
- Newsletters – promote your business in area newsletters through advertising, dear childcare director column, or parenting tips.
- Parent Communication – center newsletter
- Develop a brochure for your program.
- Continuous marketing of the program

- Design poster and put it up in supermarkets, shopping malls, stores, churches, libraries, laundry mats and any place people wait.
- Open House – Carnival, reward of mouth, newcomers, bring a friend, weekend activity classes, summer programs, space for meetings (Girl Scouts, NAEYC, childbirth classes).
- Give marketing materials to realtors offering free care for move-in day
- Company newsletters, bank or credit union statements
- Brochures to businesses
- Marketing cookies (bake secretaries for the local elementary school & give in box that has the centers name and logo)
- Coffee break – pack up coffee break boxes for mothers. Include cookies, packets of tea and coffee. Mothers take to work and display them on their desks.
- Caroling at area businesses
- Thank you letter from parents
- Catchy classifieds, "What did your child have for lunch today?" Follow with the menu and, "Our monthly field trips will be followed as scheduled…"
- Courting media
- Advocacy and working with professional organizations Parenting seminars
- Network with business leaders Park van/bus in highly visible place in front of meeting place.
- Work local events (women's conferences, art fairs, etc.).
- Send handwritten thank you and follow up notes.
- Return phone calls promptly.
- Be on-time for appointments and be sure to call if you are running behind.
- Join, attend and volunteer for professional organizations.
- Build and maintain an accurate database of parents and prospects.
- Send interesting news items to parents and prospects.
- Collect testimonials from satisfied parents. Print a brief synopsis of your school on the back of your business card.

- Ask satisfied parents for referrals. Send birthday, holiday and congratulation cards.
- Be consistent with image, logo and use of color.
- Contact media with meaningful news for "free" publicity.
- Donate an evening of care to charitable auctions and organizations.
- Use your stationary and formatted pages as your literature package.
- Buy your own paper to avoid a printer's mark-up.
- Use the same artwork for your #10 envelope and your mailing label.
- The more pieces you have design or printed at one time, the less it will cost per piece.
- Look for opportunities to co-op advertise with other businesses.
- Print a year's supply of base "shells" and laser print black copy in each issue.
- Produce a newsletter that prints on your existing stationery.
- Investigate exchanging services with a writer, designer or printer. Keep content and design short and simple.
- Consider postal automation discounts.
- Plan ahead to avoid rush charges.
- Be clear about your goals to avoid costly revisions.
- Ask your vendors if they have ideas for cost savings.
- Make sure the newsletter meets postal regulations for first class or bulk mailing.
- Consider using a syndicated newsletter. Use Facebook live videos
- Use Instagram stories
- Use social media that your clients are using to market your business
- You are a professional and a business owner. Remember to treat your business like a business and you will make money.

MAKING YOUR MARK – ESTABLISHING AN IDENTITY

An identity can be defined as the look and recognition factor of a program, the programs image. A program identity plan starts with the creation of a trademark or logo. Do not underestimate the importance of this step.

Many times, it constitutes one of the first impressions potential clients have of you and your program. And keep in mind that this is a long-term commitment!

Spend as much time as necessary on this step. Research, research, research to determine what it is you want to communicate. Remember that your program identity WILL communicate. Make sure it's sending the right message.

Consult with marketing professionals if necessary to determine your needs. Once created, you'll need to apply it to business cards, stationery, and envelopes. Many programs like to include a brochure in their program identity program right away. This will serve as an introduction. Follow the brochure with a promotional piece on a regular basis – every 30 to 90 days, as your marketing program dictates, and your budget allows. Set up systematic reminders, in email or postcard form, to serve as continual reminder of who you are and what you do. Other promotional pieces could include newsletters or specialty items with your logo. This is especially appropriate to mark holidays or program milestones. Every aspect of typography, imagery, and its application must be considered part of an integrated presentation. This integrated image presents the corporation to the public in a positive and memorable light.

Always present a unified visual identity and apply it to all of your promotional pieces. The identity program must be flexible enough to adapt to future needs.

GIVING YOURSELF A GRAPHIC OVERHAUL

If you are happy with the image you're projecting and it's working for your business, then great! Maybe it's time to apply your identity to other advertising materials, such as websites, social media, newsletters or brochures. If not, maybe it's time for a graphic overhaul. Consider the following factors when redesigning or redesigning your identity.

Type:

- Do the typeface choices reflect the nature of your program?

- Is the type legible?
- Seek a type that is appropriate to the audience and/or publication.
- Is the letter spacing appropriate?
- Does important information stand out?

Color:

- Do the graphics add to the overall message or are they just put there, actually detracting from or diminishing your message?

In General:

- Eliminate clutter and produce a clearly articulate design.
- The choice of type, graphic, illustration and/ or colors must communicate the essence of your business.
- Your logo is often reproduced in many different sizes. Your design must remain legible and strong in all circumstances.
- Because your logo may be reproduced in newspaper ads or with limited duplicating facilities, it must reproduce well in one color

Many trademarks are seen in adverse viewing conditions, such as short exposure, poor lighting, competitive surroundings, etc. Under such conditions, simplicity is a virtue. A viewer bothered by bad elements will pay less attention to the quality or content of the message. Once again, be consistent in design, intent and purpose.

Branch Out

Ask 4 people, who aren't associated with your program, to look at pictures of your signage and the outside of your building and tell you what they would expect, based on just that.

SECTION IV

Where Do You Get Your Map?

Whether you think you can, or you think you can't , you are right–
Mark Twain

In the mid 1900 there was an amazing organization. This organization marshaled every possible resource to fulfill its mission. They got people around the country to bring all their skill to bear. The president was involved; the school children were involved. It went across from one side of the country to the other, from the youngest to the most influential. They were going to eliminate a dread disease. Fast forward: they succeeded. Normally when you have achieved your mission then you stop working on the project. The problem was they had all of these people who were working inside this organization, and they had all of this organizational structure. They didn't want it to go to waste. So, they picked another mission. Many people still donate and support this organization, but it no longer has the power to capture the imagination and capture people's hearts the way the original mission driven organization did. Have you figured out the name of the organization yet? I'll bet you dimes to donuts that you know this organization. You may even have donated to it. Or marched in one of their fundraising marches.

The organization's name is the **March of Dimes.**

The March of Dimes was originally founded to raise money for medical research for the eradication of polio. The president was involved because the president was a victim of polio. Children across the country collected dimes in containers and sent them off to the March of Dimes. That is why it is called the March of Dimes. It was one of the most engaging nonprofits that the United States had ever had. Jonas Salk invented the polio vaccine and there was no longer a need for an organization to raise money to eliminate polio.

The organization had followed their business plan. They had met their goals. Instead of wrapping up the organization and moving on to other things they decided to abandon their old business plan and reinvent themselves with a new mission. Do you know what it is? I had to look it up. "March of Dimes leads the fight for the health of all moms and babies. We believe that every baby deserves the best possible start. Unfortunately, not all babies get one. We are changing that."

When you do not have a business plan, you can end up going in totally random directions that do not serve your original core values. International Business Machines still makes business machines for people all over the world. When they began, they made cash registers and adding machines. They have been through many iterations since then, but they have stayed true to their core business plan into their core mission. Recently IBM decided they needed to spin off one of their most profitable divisions, because it didn't fit their core business. That new business will go on to bigger and better things and IBM will continue to serve the business community with machinery.

I want you to be IBM not March of Dimes. That means you need a business plan. Your business plan does not have to be a huge 50-page document that is spiral-bound and is taken to investors because you're trying to get capital investment. It can be a two-page document that where you write down what the needs of your community are (assessing the situation), your key goals for the next 125 years, and the steps you're going to take to reach them. If this sounds familiar it is. It's a curriculum. You have an assessment, goals and activities. A business plan is just your way of supporting your growing and developing as a business.

How do we assess where you are? You have balance sheets. You look at the enrollment. You look at your conversion numbers: how many tours are turning into enrollments. You look at how long are people staying with your program once they enroll. If they start in your youngest age group, are they staying through the end of your program or are they all falling out in the three-year-old classroom or the four-year-old classroom? You walk through your facility with a fresh pair of eyes. That may mean that you ask someone not associated with your school to walk the building as if they were looking to buy it or looking to enroll their child. Invite the most nitpicky clean freak friends that you know or perhaps the most organized person you know or even someone who has a great eye for design to walk through your building to see what they think needs to be updated. Talk to your teachers about the curriculum. Is it serving the needs of the children? Work with them to determine what holes there are in the resources you have for the classroom: curriculum, equipment, etc. Look at your signage. Look at your marketing. Is it doing the job? This might take you one day, or it may take you two weeks. It depends on your program and what needs to be assessed. Put it into your calendar use your tiger time and get this done.

Once you know where you are, decide what you think actually *does* need to be changed. You take all the feedback from your friends who came and toured the program, from your teachers, from your budget, from your marketing results and figure out what needs to be changed. Make your goal. Outline new plans of attack. Not everything needs to be done this year. Your playground may need to be refreshed soon but not now. If that's the case, you may have these long-term projects like putting in new floors or updating your playground that you need to save for. That is a long-term goal. It might take you two or three years to save the money to completely redo the flooring in your building. That is okay. You brainstormed all the possible things that need to get done and then you pick out the ones that are the highest priority the ones that are going to be needle movers.

Once you have the short-term and long-term goals, you lay out steps like we did back in goal setting. What is the timeline for each of these items? How much is it going to cost? Who can help you? All these questions are part of your business plan. Putting together your resource team for each of your goals. Once we've got a deadline, resources, and steps we have a functional goal.

You pull your goals together write him up on paper with pen or on the computer or some programs even make up a poster. It doesn't matter. If you use a binder for your business plan, that's fabulous. If you use a poster, that's fabulous. Just make a plan and look at it. That is what a business plan is. Business Plan (small business – if you are a nonprofit – see strategic plan in the workbook)

As we have discussed in other sections, goals and plans are important in various areas of business and program management. If you are not the owner, you need to become acquainted with the owner's business plan. This assures that their plan is what you understand the "business" goals of the organization to be. If the owner and Director are not on the same page, it can cause undue stress.

A business plan should be reviewed regularly, at least annually. The business plan is designed to be a living document. If you are a director for an outside owner, ask if they have one. If not, help them find the resources to develop one. This should not be an online or software package. Most cities have Chamber of Commerce organizations that can steer your owner in the direction of appropriate resources. A business plan should include:

- The statement of purpose
- The table of contents
- Description of business
- Product or service
- Management plan
- Operations plan
- Risk
- Marketing plan
- Market, location, competition, industry analysis
- Financial data

Sources and application of funding, capital equipment list, balance sheets, break-even analysis, income projections (Profit & Loss), three-year summary, detail by month for first year and quarterly for the second and third years. Notes of explanation. Cash Flow projection: detailed by month for first year, detailed by quarters for second and third years.

Historical financial reports: balance for past three years, incomes statements.

Branch Out

Block out 2 days in your schedule, (for TIGER TIME) to work on business planning. Then do it!

CHAPTER 23

Who Makes Me Successful?

"Your network is your net worth."—Unknown

"Instead of better glasses, your network gives you better eyes." –
Ronald Burt

Truer words may never have been spoken.

I had a loan on a commercial building, and the bank had the option to adjust the interest rate every three years. I had a great relationship with the bank's branch manager. I went inside frequently, at least once a month, to make deposits and visit with the staff. Whenever things improved or worsened for us financially, I let him know. I attended bank-sponsored events and even events for the nonprofit that the bank manager personally supported. So, when it was time for our loan to be re-evaluated, the branch manager helped me put together all of the material for the loan committee. He sent documents back to me, suggesting changes that would help improve the committee's impression. He also ensured that the paperwork was submitted to the loan committee well in advance of the due date. So, when the loan committee finally met and suggested a loan rate that was higher than we had paid before, the branch manager advocated on behalf of my business and got the interest rate decreased by a half a percent. On a $300,000 commercial property, that was a difference of $15,500. Really, this was not hard to do. Once a month I walked into the bank with my checks, spent five minutes smiling and chatting with some nice people, got my complimentary lollipop from the bowl, and left. Twice, maybe three times a year, I spent a Saturday attending a very pleasant event. Five minutes every month and a couple of Saturdays a year is worth $15,500, don't you think?

Intentional networking with the people that handled my biggest liability paid off big-time. Clearly, strengthening relationships with licensing representatives, regulators, competitors, and colleges has no downside. But I can hear the age-old refrain: *"But I don't have time for all that."* We're all friends now, so please let me be blunt. We all have the same amount of time, so that makes *"I don't have time"* an outright lie. I am not being harsh, just pointing out a very limiting and possibly detrimental belief. Seriously, how much time can $15,500 buy? We want people to know that we run fabulous centers, and we want very much to enjoy this fabulous job. However, we simply cannot fulfill these two priorities if we refuse to talk to people who don't work for us. When the COVID-19 pandemic hit, I'm sure we all noticed how hard it is to really enjoy life when cut off from the wider community. Even still, I saw so many directors voluntarily social distancing within their own programs and essentially cutting themselves off from their own staff and communities.

Networking with Regulators

Our fire department, health department, and licensing agency are full of people who are habitually treated as intrusions. These regulators are painfully aware that very few people light up when they appear at the door, but it's these folks who work to ensure the safety of our centers and

our community. They also have access to information about what other folks are doing. Not only does this make them amazing people, but it also makes them amazing contacts. So by all means, network with them. Get to know them. Offer them a drink when they arrive. Ask them how they want the relevant files organized. Ask them for their opinion about a pertinent issue. Having an actual relationship as opposed to needing to ask for identification will make all the difference when there really is an issue to be handled. I personally know of two centers investigated by the same inspector for the same violation, and each received a radically different outcome: one received technical assistance while the other was put on probation. Any guess as to which one treated the visits as intrusions and which one welcomed and worked with the inspector?

If an inspector is part of your network, she is more likely to talk about the systems in our programs that need to be addressed since she sees many centers and knows what works best. Let her be your extra eyes.

Networking with the Faith-Based Community

Having relationships with nearby faith organizations is another great way to widen our networks and improve our programs. Whether those faith organizations match the religious leanings of our clientele or not, it can still impact your program positively. These organizations may have space available for us to use for big events. When we deal with a moral dilemma, these contacts make an excellent sounding board. We can partner together on community-wide events. They bring cultural diversity into our programs. We can support them in their charitable works, involving our children so that they can give back and make the world a better place. If the local church, temple, or synagogue is having a canned food drive, our programs can participate as well. Children love the idea of bringing in cans to help people who don't have enough food. Children are sensitive to those they've seen who have less than they do, and this allows them to make a difference. By combining the work of our program with that of nearby faith communities, we have a larger impact. Also, faith-based communities frequently know of people who are looking for employment. We may be able to advertise in their bulletins when we have staff openings. Church staff may call to say that there is a new member of their community who is looking for employment and they think would be a good fit. We serve their community as a place for their families to enroll their children, a place they trust will be sensitive to their values. Such connections can enrich your curriculum, and I recommend making as many of them as possible.

Networking with Area Businesses

Having relationships with nearby businesses can be another win-win situation. These businesses have employees who may have children, and a positive relationship with our programs means that they are more likely to bring their children to us. Likewise, we have clients who buy food and clothes, eat out at restaurants, and go to movies and fun parks. We have clients for them, and they have clients for us. Additionally, these businesses may do things that are interesting to the children at our schools. Children are fascinated by what happens in a dentist's office when they're not there. They would love to see how different the kitchen is in a big restaurant from the kitchens in their houses. For those businesses, it is quite an ego boost to see how enthralled the children are with the work that they do. Don't believe me? Just talk to someone who works in sanitation control—Trash men are heroes. Children love trash trucks and the people who work around them. Every person I have ever known who worked in that field shared stories of children they met who absolutely made their day. The same is true for firefighters, police officers, and chefs, so seek them out. They secretly relish the attention.

Networking with Professionals

Specialized professionals should also be part of our network. Whom do we know who works in law? Is there a pediatrician we can chat with? Look at the skills we need to grow our programs and work on getting to know people in those industries. I have friends who work at the Child Care Block Grant Agency in my area as well as librarians, realtors, HR specialists, and contractors. We will definitely want to get to know area printers and designers since we'll need a good one to finish our wonderful marketing materials. When it comes to different types of professional people to add to our network, the possibilities are truly endless.

Networking with Other Centers

The last area of networking is getting to know the other childcare programs and schools in the area. Way back in the chapter on parallel parents, we discussed how important it was to find clients who were a good match for our programs and not to enroll families who were not a match for our programs. However, when a parent is not a good match for our program, they are still going to need care somewhere. By knowing the other programs in the area, we can refer them to a program that is a better match for their needs. This will not only serve that family, but it will make us stick in their minds as a program that actually cares about the well-being of children and their families. In addition, if we have positive relationships with the other centers in our area, we can combine our efforts on important projects like annual staff trainings. If three centers are working together to hire outside trainers for their staff, then they can afford better ones more often if each center pitches in. We can also opt to train each other's staff, rotating through the year with each center presenting choice topics. That way we can have much of the required annual training handled in-house. It is also courteous to let the other centers know when we have a client who is not paying their bills. If we tell them about clients who are not paying their bills, then they will likely do the same for us. Protecting each other from the bad actors in the crowd is a benefit for all. So it comes down to this: the more plugged in we are to the wider community, the more diverse our network will be. Choose to cultivate this diverse network and watch the myriad ways our programs will grow and thrive. And we all know that a thriving program equals joy and success for those blessed to be called directors.

Branch Out

Make a list of your current network and at least 20 other people or organizations you would like to add to your network.

CHAPTER 24

What Does My Center Stand For?

"If you stand for nothing, what'll you fall for?"
—Lin Manuel-Miranda

We are complete persons. Each of us has an intellectual life, a physical life, financial life, professional life, and a spiritual life. The definition of a spiritual life varies greatly based on the individual, but every human being wants to know that by doing what they do, they make the world a better place. Just by nature of working in childcare, we are advocates. As far as child and family health are concerned, we can kick our advocacy up a notch by being even more targeted in what we're advocating for. One of the directors I worked with took this the heart. She wanted to open a childcare center because she wanted to do for other families what had been done for her. In particular, the center that her had child attended when she was young had a monthly health focus: one month was heart health; the next, nutrition; another, breast cancer; following that, physical activity and so on. With each topic, the center engaged parents with different types of communication and education. During the month when breast cancer awareness was highlighted, they sent home information about how to do a breast self-exam. Having never done a breast self-exam and guided by the materials, she decided to go ahead and do one. She found a lump. After having it diagnosed and treated, today she is healthy and without challenges. And she credits that center with saving her life. At this woman's center, child and family health will be the core elements of her business. She has a larger advocacy issue than simply child welfare.

As directors of programs serving families, we have the potential to make significant changes in the community. We can work to increase funding for research into childhood diseases, broaden public transportation options, decrease advertising directed at young children, or increase funding for education at various levels. Perhaps we are concerned with support for small business or litigation reform. We represent a powerful force in the economies of our communities. This means we can work with others to improve the lives of our clients, their children, and our employees.

We can move the world toward our advocacy goals. Archimedes said, *"If you give me a long enough lever, I could lift the world."* The more people who work an issue, the longer the lever is. What Does Advocacy Mean? Advocacy is the process whereby people mobilize to communicate a message to a targeted audience. In this case, the audience is the elected officials who serve us. The future of early childhood and school-age programs lies in the level of commitment that public officials take to fund these programs. Our voices, in turn, impact their level of commitment.

The future of our children also depends on how we take care of them and teach them to grow, so what is our message? Our message to elected officials must convey that in today's society, school-age and early childhood programs keep kids safe, help working families, and improve academic achievement. An accompanying message may be to convince them that it is in the people's best interest to support these school-age and early childhood programs financially.

Whatever the message, it is is our responsibility to get the message out, and it is the duty of elected officials to respond. If the issue doesn't require governmental intervention, then whom do we need to influence?

For those of us working in programs receiving federal grants, please bear in mind that federal funding may not be used to lobby elected officials. We can, however, communicate the successes of our programs and hope for continued support.

Tips for Contacting Policy Makers.
Here are simple principles of advocacy, courtesy of www.afterschoolalliance.org:

1. Consider yourself an expert information source. Elected officials have limited time, staff, and many competing issues to deal with every day. They cannot be as well informed as those actually implementing or witnessing the programs. You can fill their information gap and be their "expert."

2. Always tell the truth. Make your word impeccable.

3. Know who is on your side. This is your strength. The elected official will want to know this.

4. Know who is not on your side. The elected official will want to know who stands against your issue. Anticipate the opposition arguments and provide the answers and the rebuttals.

5. Make the elected official aware of any personal connections you may have. If you have friends, relatives, or colleagues in common with an elected official let them know. This is how we connect with one another.

6. Admit you don't know something. It gives you a reason to follow-up with the official after you have researched an answer.

7. Be specific. Tell the official what you want. Ask them directly. Expect a direct answer in response.

8. Follow-up. The elected official should be held accountable for any statements they make to you. Find out if the official took action. Then thank them for any action they took and make your next request.

Over the years we have worked with centers whose advocacy issues cover a wide range of topics. Some programs focus on outdoor education, others, the benefits of bilingual education. In fact, one of the most memorable was a program focusing on the arts with theatre, sculpting, and dance programs.

What Do I Stand For?

What about you? What do you want to stand for? Pinpoint that, and advocacy is a way to narrow that focus with laser-sharp precision. Advocacy also carries the beneficial side effects of informing your curriculum and aiding with staff retention. If you are advocating for arts education, then lesson plans will reflect this emphasis. Teachers who know that they are changing the world are more likely to stay, which is why Fortune 500 companies are adding social impact projects to their annual schedule. Advocacy events like an end-of-the-year showcase make excellent publicity events.

For forever or just for this year, find your advocacy issue. Discover what you stand for.

Branch Out

Brainstorm possible advocacy focuses with members of your leadership team.

CHAPTER 25

Who Will Be My Cheerleader?

"I absolutely believe that people, unless coached, never reach their maximum capabilities."
—*Bob Nardelli*

One thing you probably don't know about me is that I am a huge basketball nerd. I have my favorites, but let's discuss someone everyone might recognize: Michael Jordan. Most people don't know that Michael Jordan did not make the basketball team when he first started. He just wasn't talented, they thought. Instead of getting discouraged, Michael asked the coach what he could do to make the team the next time, and the coach said practice. So he practiced and practiced, and in time Michael was good enough to get on the team. But he still wasn't the best. Once he was on the team, he asked the coach how to get faster. The coach gave him drills to get faster, and he practiced those daily. By the time he went to college, Michael was both fast enough and talented enough to get picked for a first-tier basketball team, North Carolina State. But he still wasn't the best.

He asked his new coach what he had to do to be as good as the senior guys. The coach told him that he needed to practice his layup shots, so he came in every day and spent an hour practicing his layups. His layups improved so much that the coach gave him more time on the court, but it wasn't good enough for Michael. He wasn't achieving what he thought he could achieve. So, he went back to his coaches again. This time the coach said Michael needed to do more and more drills. He worked every day, an hour before practice and another after. By the time he graduated from college, he was drilling up to four hours every day in addition to the basketball practices and arose as one of the best college basketball players, but that wasn't good enough for Michael. He still wasn't the best.

He was drafted onto a team that was the joke of the league. The Chicago Bulls had not won a championship or even gone to the playoffs in years, and Michael declared that he wanted to take this team to the playoffs. Of course, everyone said that this brash young kid from North Carolina was just talking crazy. After years of working with one coach after another, Michael Jordan emerged as the quintessential NBA player and led the Chicago Bulls to not one but six NBA championships, an unprecedented feat in the history of the game. How did Michael accomplish all this? He sought out good coaches and remained coachable.

There were plenty of other people on Michael Jordan's teams, but I'll bet that not all of them listened to their coaches. Many probably made excuses as to why they couldn't do what the coaches were asking. Maybe they were too short. Maybe they were tired. Maybe they had never played that certain way before. However, the same could be said for Michael Jordan. He was not the tallest. He did not have a lot of leisure time. In fact, he had never even played triangle basketball before, but he was coachable. Because of that, he did indeed become the best.

We can be amazing directors. We can have profitable centers full of happy, engaged staff and above-average children, but we can't do it on our own. Each of us needs a coach, someone who unlocks the gym for us and tells us what drills we need to run… someone who has been there, done that, and succeeded. It doesn't matter if we call that person a coach or a mentor. What is important is that we seek out successful business leaders, especially those in our chosen field, and ask for help. We have to be coachable.

Seeking Out a Good Coach

Good coaches and mentors will help take our programs to the highest levels, and we may benefit from more than one. Some may be the authors of books whose knowledge and experience we read, process, and most importantly implement. They may be people met through volunteer organizations like SCORE or the Chamber of Commerce. They may be coaches hired to help improve specific areas of our businesses. They may be executive coaches who come in to help design systems and structures grow the program to the next level. While I cannot specify who will be needed to fill this role, I will emphatically state that this role cannot be left unfilled.

However, I can specify who should *not* fill this role: our parents, our spouses, and our staff. More importantly, they probably don't want to. Parents are there to be supportive. Spouses or significant others are there to love us, especially on the days when we're crabby. Staff are there to help with our vision, but it's not their job to help fine-tune it. That has to be someone else. We need someone who is not within our organizations, someone who can see a broader picture.

First, start by reading books. Find people whose message resonates with you. Then seek out coaches or mentors whose philosophy and approach also resonate with those messages. If everything written by Dr. Maria Montessori resonates, then find a mentor who has successfully run a stellar Montessori program. If Brené Brown or Tony Robbins resonates, then find discussion groups to help channel and apply that knowledge. We have to actively seek out people who light us up and then let them coach us into being the best version of ourselves.

Branch Out

Pick one area of your life or business where you need coaching. Find your first coach.

CHAPTER 26

Are My Assets Covered?

"The most exciting environments, that treated people very well, are also tough as nails. There is no bureaucratic mumbo-jumbo...excellent companies provide two things simultaneously: tough environments and very supportive environments."
—Tom Peters

Ours is not a super-risky business, but risks are involved. Sometimes we don't see them coming. I know I didn't see them coming in my relationship with Kiki. Kiki was a long-time staff person at a center that I purchased. I really enjoyed her, and I initially considered her as an asset to the program. What I did not expect was her morphing into a huge liability for my business.

She was the lead teacher in my largest classroom. She also had two children at the center for which she received discounted childcare. While everything appeared to be going very well during this transition, I was not aware that Kiki was deeply unhappy. She had not-so-secretly hoped to buy the business herself but was financially unable to do so. Because of this, she set on a course that almost torpedoed the entire center.

Kiki suddenly decided that my policies did not match her needs, and she let everyone know about it. In her anger and frustration, she spread half-truths to other staff members as well as the parents. In fact, she got them so upset that half of her very large class of twenty-seven children was on the verge of withdrawing from the center entirely. The loss of half of that class would have made it impossible to continue my loan payments associated with buying the center, and the nature of her half-truths to people made it difficult for me to respect confidentiality. In this case, Kiki represented three significant risks: increased expenses in the form of free childcare for her family, breaches of confidentiality, and a financial loss from clients leaving the program. Fortunately, I was able to resolve this issue without actually suffering any of the potential downsides, but it took a lot of work to do that. The only reason I made it through that difficult situation was that I had good policies, good documentation, good communication, and some darn good insurance.

We won't necessarily be able to spot every risk in our businesses. Some things may look like opportunities but end up being huge dangers. The best way to avoid having any shiny objects, colorful people, or random happenstance derail your business is to prepare for the risks.

Childcare centers are rarely involved in lawsuits, and they are rarely the victims of crime or scams. As slim as some risks may be, they remain real possibilities. To be good businesswomen, we must do our best to prepare for potential dangers. It is not my job to go over every possible risk factor, and I'm not trying to scare you here at the end of the book. Rather, I place this chapter here because it is something we think about at the end, an afterthought. Once everything it set up and running wonderfully, then we think about how to protect it.

Risks Involving Employees

Employees are probably the biggest risk factors, and they are covered by more laws than we could possibly cover in this book. When employees are upset over a work situation or a work separation, it is a most beneficial to have an ongoing relationship with an human relations (HR) manager or subscribe to a service that provides information with up-to-date HR regulations. This is one reason why many centers choose to use a payroll service like ADP, which helps avoid many of the potential liabilities incumbent upon having employees. A relationship with an HR professional will help ensure that the right signs are posted that the staff receives appropriate guidance, that the right questions are asked during interviews, and that the wrong questions are avoided altogether. We also have to protect ourselves from claims of discrimination, favoritism, and lack of support. Making sure that all of the potential policy issues outlined in staff handbook are covered is key to protection from these liabilities. Specifically, sexual misconduct, competition, dating, and maintaining a culturally and gender-appropriate dress code are paramount concerns.

Staff may not do what you have trained them to do every single time. An employee may walk away from a child on a changing table. Another may go out for lunch with a friend and have a margarita before coming back to work. We simply cannot foresee all of the bad choices our staff may make. Nevertheless, many of these choices are potential liabilities for us as directors and for our centers. Therefore, our job is to have clear policies and adhere to them. If it is policy that a person who appears unable to do her work must leave the center, go to a doctor, and be cleared before coming back, then Margarita Girl has to comply. Not only will she not be getting paid for that afternoon, but she now has to pay for a doctor's visit—because that is what the policy says. However, if that is not what is explicitly written in the policy, we cannot legally require her to get alcohol tested. Our hands are tied.

On the other hand, if policy states that random and with-cause drug and alcohol testing is at the discretion of the director, then the first line of action will be drug and alcohol testing anytime an employee seems unable to do her work. Not only do we need to enforce these policies, but we also need to document w=every time we enforce them. When writing up what occurred, do so as objectively as possible such as: *"Teacher A came back from lunch. She was walking unevenly, her breath smelled unusual, and her speech was not clear. Therefore, we sent her to the doctor to be cleared for return to work."* Follow the policies, document that the policies were followed, and notify the insurance company when relevant. If a teacher was in this impaired state when a child is injured, notify your insurance company immediately. If the insurance company is notified of the issue, then they are prepared to defend the center if any legal action occurs, or the child requires medical care. These three elements together: insurance, policies, and documentation are the best defense against employee misbehavior and misconduct.

In my situation with Kiki, her misconduct rose to another type of employee risk: behavior which causes families to disenroll in the program. Employees may chase clients away with foul language, inappropriate jokes, or blatant failure to do their jobs properly. They might even pull parents out of the center by setting up a rival program in their own house or at another school. I've had both of these happen over the years, and it is painful. But because I was prepared, it was not terminal. We may also choose to have an employment agreement with your teachers that includes a non-compete clause. This ensures that teachers who leave to set up their own programs or to work for someone else cannot poach your clients without financial redress. This does mean being willing and ready to take them to small claims court, should the need arise. Fortunately, good relationships with clients allow them to bring their concerns about poor employee performance to us as directors, allowing us a chance to fix the problem. In the Kiki situation, the parents did bring it to my attention, and I was then able to share our policies. Almost all of them remained with our program. Incidentally, ensuring that all of our eggs are not in one financial basket is key to weathering any storm related to withdrawals. If most of our clients come from one employer, we stand to lose a huge percentage of our clientele over a single incident. Therefore, our earlier discussion about business diversification is actually a form of insurance as well.

Risks Involving Accidents

Accidents are going to happen at our centers. They will happen to our staff. They will happen to the children. They may even happen to the parents who are bringing their children to school. Because of this, we need insurance. Basically, insurance is legalized gambling and is legal all over the world. The insurance company is betting that people will not need to use the insurance; when we purchase coverage, we are betting that we will.

For any area in which insurance is not purchased, we should consider ourselves self-insured. Since very few insurance agents specialize in insuring childcare businesses, they may try and sell us products that we may not need and fail to offer us resources that we should have. To get a leg up in these conversations, let's briefly address the kinds of coverage available:

- General limits of liability up to $1,000,000 per occurrence / $3,000,000 aggregate
- Teacher Professional Liability
- Sexual Abuse & Molestation coverage
- Corporal Punishment Liability
- Optional endorsements on your liability policy, including:
  - » 1. Medical Personnel Liability
  - » 2. Child Abduction Liability
  - » 3. Directors' and Officers' Liability
  - » 4. General Liability Extension Endorsement
  - » 5. Employment Practices Liability
- Accidental Medical Payments is a feature of Business Interruption Insurance. It functions such that you are covered for day care children's accidental injuries up to $5,000 per accident with a zero deductible to the provider. Coverage is considered primary, meaning that we do not ask the parent to present the claim to their medical carrier before we will pay the claim. Coverage is no-fault and is applied to necessary items such as first aid, medical, surgical, dental services, ambulance, hospital, and professional nursing services. Exclusions are the children's eyewear.
- Additional Insured for our family members.
- Business Interruption Insurance is a time-element coverage that pays for loss of earnings when operations are curtailed or suspended because of property loss due to an insured peril. A Business Owner Policy works in these three ways:
  - » 1. Defends you if you are sued related to your childcare operations.

» 2. Pays for medical expenses for day care children's trip and fall with zero deductible.

» 3. Pays for your loss of business income due to necessary suspension of your operations caused by: fire, smoke, windstorm, hail, falling objects, or bursting of pipes. All of this coverage requires no waiting period, no set limit, and up to a 12 month period of recovery.

- General Aggregate Limit is a commercial general liability limit that applies to all damages paid for bodily injury, property damage, personal injury, advertising injury, and medical expenses except damages included in the products-completed operations hazard.

- Liability Insurance pays and renders service on behalf of an insured for loss arising out of his or her responsibility to others imposed by law or assumed by contract.

- Occurrence Coverage provides liability coverage only for injury or damage that occurs during the policy period, regardless of when the claim is actually made. For example, a claim made in the current policy year could be charged against a previous policy year, or may not be covered, if it arises from an occurrence prior to the effective date.

- Professional Liability Insurance functions such that the insurance company will provide first dollar defense by providing legal protection to the insured for anything they do, don't do, or do in error. Limits start at $300,000 and are consistent with the General Liability limit chosen.

- Umbrella Liability offers extra liability insurance, above your primary liability and auto policies. This coverage is designed to protect you and your assets in the event of a catastrophic accident.

- Property insurance covers damage to; buildings, personal property, equipment and contents caused by specific perils, like: fire, lightning, explosions, windstorms and hail, smoke, aircraft or vehicles, vandalism and more (as named in the policy).

» Coverage for playground equipment, fences and signs.

» Optional coverage's include Commercial Property Extension, Business Income
- Communicable Disease and Food Contamination Coverage
- Key Employee
- Replacement Coverage
- Crime Coverage protects against the potential dishonest acts of employees who handle checks, money, merchandise, or equipment at the facility or in the office as well as theft or burglary of money or securities.
- System Breakdown protects from the perils of mechanical and electrical breakdown to all covered electrical, mechanical, and pressure systems equipment. It also covers loss from a boiler explosion if there happens to be a boiler present. Any interruption in day-to-day operations can mean a tremendous loss of dollars, plus the additional expense for repairs to damaged equipment.
- Commercial Automobile covers owned, leased, non-owned and hired automobiles such as vans, pickups, and buses used at your facility. If you don't own any vehicles, then use the Unowned Vehicle Insurance rider on your liability insurance.
- Accidental Death & Dismemberment, limit options up to $10,000
- Workman's Compensation Insurance, covering injuries and illness incurred in the workplace

Make sure that the building's liability insurance covers the entire time people are in the building, including before the center is open and after the center is closed. When staff arrive 30 minutes before the school opens and parents are 30 minutes late picking up, we need to ensure that the coverage is in place. during those time. The same goes for special evening or weekend events. Some policies are tied strictly to your license and do not protect you outside of licensed care hours.

Our playgrounds have the biggest potential for physical accidents. Things to climb on, things to swing on, things to jump off, and room to run all of these are potentially risky activities. They are also necessary activities because children require plenty of gross motor play and risk-taking behaviors.

However, that behavior needs to be wrapped in a bubble of policies and documentation. What should the teachers be directing the children to do on the equipment? What are the playground rules? Ensure that the play equipment is appropriate to the ages of children who are playing on that playground. Post the playground rules so that teachers can have a visual reminder of what is expected on this playground. When a child or staff person gets hurt on the playground, there should be a document trail. A form is filled out as soon as possible explaining what happened and why it happened. If a child was injured, then one copy of that document a goes to the parent, and a second copy goes into the confidential files. Accident reports should be reviewed once a month to see if there are any new trends. New trends might lead to new policies and employee training.

If an accident involves an employee, we have a different set of forms to fill out which may include workman's compensation insurance. This insurance pays for medical care and time off for employees who are hurt in the workplace. Our workman's compensation insurance will be lower if we have good policies and good documentation.

Risks Involving Parents

The parents of the children at your center are indeed a risk, but one we cannot live without. We need people to pay for our service. The most likely parent-related liability is a call to the licensing agency with a concern. This usually happens when we do not have clear grievance policy set up in our handbook or outlined in our new family orientation or they believe that they have found reason not to trust us. Either way, there needs to be a way for parents to express a concern and get a reasonable response back from the management. Simply saying, "I will talk to the teacher about it" is not an appropriate response in itself. Of course, we can say that we'll talk to the teacher, but we then need to actually do it and then inform the parent of the plan of action. Only then is the concern fully remedied. There should also be a way to submit concerns or complaints anonymously. If we receive an anonymous complaint, then we must resolve the issue, write up what was done, and post it in a place where the anonymous parent is likely to see it and read it such as a newsletter or the classroom bulletin board. Be upfront and authentic. Occasionally we may have litigious parents. Parents made threaten to sue the center about not treating their child with a disability in the appropriate manner, about discrimination, or even about an employee's misconduct. This is the primary reason why we need the insurance we discussed earlier. Additionally, we need to have good documentation about how our policies and procedures are implemented and maintained. I have been working in childcare for more than 25 years and have never been party to such a lawsuit. They are very rare if you have open and clear communication and you are consistent, but they are possible.

The only legal actions involving parents that I have been party to multiple times are legal separation, divorce, or custody battles. If we operate our centers for any significant length of time, we will have a family unit that dissolves. To protect our assets, we should stay out of these situations whenever possible. Some parents do not respect the fact that we want to stay out of their business. Parents may want to subpoena the staff, they may request documents for their legal team, or they may try to get us to personally take sides in the disagreement. This is another place where the policies can save our bacon. Simply add lines to the parent handbook stating that any copies of documents will have a fee associated with them and that any legal testimony by staff will incur an expert witness fee. We do not have to specify what that document fee is or how much the expert witness fee is. We just need to notify them that it exists. The specific amount should be in your SOP. This way you do not have to change your entire handbook if you need to increase the cost of either of these rarely used fees. This will discourage overuse of the center as a document source for the legal proceedings and keep any subpoenaing of staff to the bare minimum. Related to this is the changing of child pick-up. I am not a lawyer, and I do not take play one on TV, so please consult with one if ever in a situation related to child custody or relationship dissolution. My understanding is that in most cases the parent or guardian that is listed first on the enrollment paperwork is considered be managing parent or guardian. That means if there is a conflict between the two parents as to who can pick up the children, the first parent or guardian's decision reigns. If a situation arises where the child's parents are governed by custody agreement or a custody order and they ask the center to enforce these orders, we will need:

An original notarized copy of those orders, and To call the police department anytime a parent is violating the orders. Only officers of the Court can enforce court orders. A police officer or sheriff is an officer of the court. You and your staff are not. Parents should handle these disagreements without involving us because we cannot legally correct the situation.

Risks Involving Environment

The last category of risks is environmental risks, which includes all natural disasters. Pandemics, floods, wildfires, and major storms all have the potential to seriously damage the operation of our businesses. Ensuring that we have the correct insurance for each of these occurrences is imperative. While we do not need insurance for all of them, we do need insurance for the ones that are most likely to occur at our program. If you live in a coastal area, having flood and hurricane insurance is just good business. Talk over the potential risks with the insurance agent and select the ones that are appropriate for the program.

Insurance is also there to protect you in case of a crime. If the center is vandalized or broken into, this would come into play to cover the cost of repairing or replacing the damaged items.

The last type of environmental change is the financial environment. If there is a recession or a depression, this will affect the number of families that can pay for our services. If the neighborhood becomes popular with retirees, they will have very little need for childcare. Both of these are examples of environmental changes that will affect our businesses. Pay attention to what is happening in the local economy and with local demographics. The more diverse our income streams are, the lower the risk. Looking at these once a quarter will help us pivot when we need to pivot and even relocate if necessary.

Covering assets just takes a little bit of forward-thinking. I find talking to my local cynic to be of enormous help in figuring out what might be risks I could encounter in my center. Talk through potential dangers with others, devise a good list, create a policy document addressing these situations, and purchase insurance for what you need. That's all we have to do.

Branch Out

Determine which types of insurance you must have and which ones you might want to learn more about.

CHAPTER 27

Grow Out and Get Them!

"Thunder is good, thunder is impressive, but it is the lightning that does all the work."   *–Mark Twain*

We have reached the end of our journey together. Now is the time for you to grow out in the world and make a difference. No, that is not a typo. I want you to grow out. I want you to continue to grow and develop and evolve. This job, Early Childhood Director, is the most magical job I can imagine. You get to change the way the world will be in 20 years. The children that you help to nurture will go out into the world to make it the world we want it to be.

Go through whatever licensing procedure you need to go through in order to get qualified to be a director. If you're in Texas, that is the course that this book is based on. If you are somewhere else and you want my help, reach out to me I will help to connect you with people who can support you in your journey to be a quality director.

Take a stand in your program. Require that people respect your time and your expertise. Appreciate your Tiger Time. Reach out to your network. Take joy in the developmental milestones of the children in your program.

Nurture your staff to be the best they can be. Find families who want the type of program that you can offer. Do great things!

Branch Out

Create a vision board of what you want your world to be like in two years.